The Correct Way To Fool Around Part IV
By Jeremiah Dotson

Corrections P.179
            P.161
            P.174
            P.102

To Mom
Best Wishes
Jeremiah Dotson

Well here it is - the fourth and as it stands now, final edition of The Correct Way To Fool Around. Most of you who know me or have read my previous works, already know that The Correct Way To Fool Around was originally meant to be nothing more than a seventy two page, alcohol fueled, weekend rant circling around many of the trifling women I have had the pleasant and sometimes not so pleasant misfortune of involving myself with. Fortunately, the topic of infidelity is not one, which can be fully explained nor even the surface scratched in a seventy two page book. For infidelity to be fully examined, it would take years upon years, scholars upon scholars, married people upon married people and books upon books. Infidelity is something, which has intrigued mankind I believe since the beginning of time and will continue to do so I believe until the end of time. Infidelity is much more than just a sin, for some it is a hobby, for others, an unrelenting obsession. To understand infidelity - what drives it or why people are compelled to commit it will take more than just a few books from me. It will take more than reading books in general. It will have to be lived, experienced, fought and destroyed before one can truly say he or she knows what the definition of infidelity really is.

Acknowledgements

A special thanks to all who supported my vision even if you never read any of the books you bought. I understand – some of my writing could be interpreted as a tad bit controversial, offensive and or sickening.

A special thank you to all of the trifling women I've dated, without whom The Correct Way To Fool Around series would have never materialized. I will not mention the names of these trifling women because many of them would not actually believe they have the capability to be trifling.

A special thank you as always to my baby Kathy – couldn't do it without you. Love ya.

I would lastly like to acknowledge the folks close to me who have had to deal with the backlash from my creative endeavors. It has come to my attention that many people do not seem to like me because of the content contained within my books. I'm sorry. I really don't care as much as I should because this is me. This is my attitude. In case you could not tell from my first book and it's acknowledgements, let me try to explain. I have had over forty jobs in one particular line of work - The reason why, I have a low tolerance for bullshit. People tell me all the time nobody will hire me with my work history and that I should learn to 'put up with the bullshit' so to speak so that life would be easier and more fruitful. I tried that. It lasted for about a month. You see when a person is forced to do something he or she does not like, that person will not be happy. If a person is not happy, he or she will usually try to make himself or herself happy. I never planned on jumping from job to job as many times as I have; it just ended up that way. People need to understand that I am not one to hide feelings – you will find out my true feelings in one way or another. And why, cause it makes me happy. Telling my employers to kiss my ass made and still makes me happy. This is what I try to get across to people in my books about relationships. People who are not happy will try almost anything to make themselves happy. This includes not calling someone back after you sleep with him or her, cheating or just leaving somebody when times get hard. What I also try to get across to people is that my words, thoughts and opinions are my own, not those of the people around me and definitely not those related to me. So if you are one of those who is in any way dissatisfied with what I write, one, don't read any more of my material and two, don't hate anybody except me.

And as always Mark & Corey - Love Ya!

Topics Of Discussion

<u>Chapter One</u> - Infidelity At Its Finest

<u>Chapter Two</u> - How Not To Get Caught

<u>Chapter Three</u> - The Correct Way To Fool Around

<u>Chapter Four</u> - Let's Stop The Bullshit

<u>Chapter Five</u> – Conquering And Being Conquered

<u>Chapter Six</u> – Infidelity; The Victim And The Perpetrator

<u>Chapter Seven</u> - An Open Mind Must Be Maintained When Confronting Or Combating Infidelity.

<u>Chapter Eight</u>
The Perfect Crime

<u>Chapter Nine</u>
Your Relationship Is What You Say It Is

<u>Chapter Ten</u>
Ramifications

<u>Chapter Eleven</u>
Possessions

<u>Chapter Twelve</u>
Complacency

<u>Chapter Thirteen</u>
The Contradictory Nature Of Relationships

<u>Chapter Fourteen</u>
More Deception

<u>Chapter Fifteen</u>
One Final Note About Cheating

Chapter One
Infidelity At Its Finest

Infidelity is one of those things, which unfortunately will never die. Not only will infidelity never die, it will never fade or go out of style. It exists on the same level as racism and prostitution, which unfortunately will never die, fade or go out of style either. Infidelity is a multifaceted entity, which provides a different service for different people in relationships. At its most basic level, infidelity is little more than the equivalent of a smash and grab robbery, where one would smash a window to a jewelry store and then grab the merchandise inside – the thrill of which would be enough to satisfy the immediate desire of any low level thief. At its most extreme level, I like to believe that infidelity is equivalent to the design of an aircraft or equivalent to that same thief using an entire year to plan a heist to perfection. Now when it comes to being unfaithful, most people have a basic working knowledge of how it can occur, when it is most likely to occur and some of the reasons why it can occur but the one thing about infidelity, which many people tend to over look is the fact that infidelity itself <u>can</u> be understood. It has a reason for being and not just the reason that most people like to believe – that those who partake in it are scumbags. Sometimes the act of cheating does have a therapeutic effect on relationships, meaning it can provide a helpful service. The services, which infidelity provides can be broken up into two main fields. The first is providing basic sexual intercourse when there is none in the committed relationship and the second is providing an out when the relationship is stagnant or ending. In any relationship that goes sour there are what's commonly called options for correction. These options for correction include professional therapy, separation and the introduction of another partner. Since professional therapy is often much more costly than most couples going through adversity can afford, the other two options are taken into consideration. Separation is highly desired but it too is often costly and the effects many times outweigh the benefits of staying together. This leaves the option of another partner. When people stay together in an unhappy relationship, it is almost a certainty that there will be little to no intimacy in the relationship. There can and many times however will be plenty of intimacy outside of the relationship. Most times this will be accomplished in secret, meaning an unhappily married man may have a woman on the side without his wife knowing about it or the unhappily married woman may have a man on the side without the husband's knowledge. Sometimes there are relationships, which entail the unhappily married husband having a girlfriend and his wife having a boyfriend (also in secret). There are some folks who go against the norm and let the significant other know that they have somebody else and that the significant other is only around for appearances or for the sake of kids. Now when another partner is used for the sake of obtaining an out from the relationship, it usually is because one partner is incapable of ending the relationship on his or her own. They are either afraid to say 'I don't love you and don't want to be with you anymore' because they fear consequences from the significant other, like physical harm or because they don't know of any other way to end the relationship.

Infidelity at its finest point occurs when no one is the wiser. By this I mean there exists or must exist an unequalled level of deception. Infidelity at its finest can occur when all parties involved know each other but are unaware that certain parties are sleeping together. The innocent party may even be best friends with the one cheating with the spouse. The cheater in a situation such as this, in an attempt to exonerate himself or herself from suspicion, will say things to the effect of you should marry him or her or he or she is a perfect catch, all while sleeping with the one who is supposed to be so perfect. Let's say for instance, a husband and wife are enjoying what seems to be an otherwise happy relationship and either the husband or the wife is carrying on a second relationship at the same time. This is not polygamy. Polygamy is having more than one spouse at the same time. This is infidelity. Infidelity, most times is a very well thought out and planned course of action, which usually only one of the parties involved in the relationship is aware of. I call this the finest point of infidelity because like I mentioned in The Correct Way To Fool Around part one, one has to be an expert at planning so that the two relationship paths don't cross. He or she also needs to be extremely proficient at budgeting so that an equal or sufficient amount of time will be allotted to both individuals. Finally, the one initiating the transgression must be able to keep each person in the relationship away from all family members of the other person in the relationship. This is almost the same as committing the perfect murder, which is impossible but a person must be able to come as close to it as possible. 'Infidelity at its finest' entails hiding one's indiscretions in plain sight. It is a woman having relations with two unaware individuals who share the same home. It is a man having sex with best friends who are both unaware. The operative phrase here is 'no one is the wiser.' It is not regular deception but the epitome of. Regular deception often entails a married person telling someone outside of the relationship he or she is looking for a discreet encounter or more and in a relationship of this sort, the person sought after usually knows to keep quiet. What follows is a true example of infidelity at its finest.

June 15th 2005, Ryan, not his real name, met Tasha, not her real name either at a Central Park restaurant for dinner. They originally met on Craig's list personals. Ryan is married and so is Tasha but neither Ryan nor Tasha's spouse paid any attention to the excessive computer usage taking place during the late night hours. They begin to email each other daily, then several times a day. The online conversations consisted mainly of tales of unhappiness between the two and stories of how no concern is being paid regarding each other's actions. It was almost inevitable that two people with so much in common would fall for each other. The online conversations gravitated from stories of unhappiness and unconcern to make believe dates and imaginary tales of how they would treat each other if ever they were in a real relationship. The make believe online world continued until Tasha suggested that she and Ryan grab lunch one day – at Tavern On The Green. Tasha told her husband that she just needed to get away and him, trying to be supportive, allows her the requested space without question. Ryan just leaves because it is something that his wife is used to. Her only concern regarding him is that he comes home with some money. What's done between the times he leaves and the time he returns is unimportant. The two of them meet for lunch and Ryan is captivated by the atmosphere and surroundings. Tasha is happy, yet unimpressed because this is the same restaurant her husband had brought her to on their first date.

The two of them talk, have dinner and reconfirm the unhappy feelings they both share. Lunch turns into dinner and the two of them end up at Ryan's job where he works as a maintenance engineer. Ryan uses the key to his bosses' office, which has a leather couch. The leather couch becomes their bed. The office becomes their private refuge. Wednesdays become their special day. Today is Wednesday, June 18th. They are at Tavern On The Green celebrating their three - year secret anniversary and yes they are both still married.

Relationships like this are not uncommon. They are what now appears to be the patchwork of American society. People these days feel that it is not only cool but also accepted as well as necessary to carry on a secondary relationship. It used to be that when a person cheated the relationship was pretty much over on the part of the woman and just a fulfilled fantasy on the part of the man. But as of late, things have progressed to the point of 'I'm not happy but I refuse to lose my entire relationship because of that fact – so I will do any and everything up to and including having a stand by husband or wife for those times when the original husband or wife pisses me off.' This is where regular infidelity is dangerous and potentially detrimental. Regular infidelity, like the smash and grab example above can entail just screwing the first person who allows you to do so – which can get you killed. The infidelity at its finest mindset will cause a person to take the necessary precautions, which will make said person do everything possible not to get caught. People in relationships want to be completely fulfilled. If there is any part of the relationship, which is lacking, these people will find a way to make up the slack. Making up the slack often includes having an extra marital affair because it is easier than attempting to work out the problems within the relationship without one.

Here's an example:

<u>WHO</u>	<u>PROBLEM</u>
Husband – mid 40's	cannot achieve and or maintain erections

SOLUTION #1
Viagra, therapy or any of the readily available male enhancement products presently on the market

SOLUTION #2
Have an affair (Wife)

Chapter Two
How Not To Get Caught

Basic principle – when something a person owns no longer works properly, that person has but three options regarding his or her next choice of action. The first is usually the most thought of option and that is to fix it. The second option people choose is the one, which occurs after all attempts at option number one have failed and that is to get rid of it. The third and final option is just as popular as the other two – only just with a certain type of people. That option entails getting a brand new one. This basic principle applies to relationships in such a way that everyone in a relationship falls into one of the above three categories. Looking at relationships with this principle, if one is not going completely according to plan, people will either attempt to remedy the problem, break up from the relationship altogether or find a new relationship. All three of these solutions are okay provided they are done in the correct manner. Some people feel the correct manner in attempting to fix a non working relationship is to automatically break up. Others think the correct manner is to find a new relationship altogether – and some even feel the proper way to fix a non working relationship is to find a new relationship in addition to the old. I would like to focus on the last group of people because they are the ones who are the basis behind The Correct Way To Fool Around. These people are the cheaters. They are the ones who risk personal harm, character assassination and financial destruction just to avoid being alone. Now unlike the other two groups of people, the cheaters have no long term plans for those they use for sex. They usually get it as much as they can, whenever they can. In other words they want to have someone at their complete disposal. Cheaters sometimes have a blatant disregard, if you will for everyone's happiness – outside of their own. As mentioned before, some of those who commit infidelity do not wish to be alone and there are others who simply cannot be alone. These are the types of people who will make your life hell! Now most of the cheaters believe it or not, do not need much provocation when it comes to the act of infidelity. Usually they already have some underlying or unresolved issue in their lives, which causes them to find difficulty when it comes to staying committed. Cheating, like many other derogatory acts in this world is easy. The power to resist is what's hard. I like to use jaywalking as an example because in some areas it is an actual violation of certain laws. The act of jaywalking consists of crossing the street in the middle of the block as opposed to walking to the corner and doing so. Anybody can walk all the way to the corner to cross the street but for one, it takes a lot more time, and two whatever it was that made you want to cross the street in the first place will be that much farther when you walk all the way down the block unless of course it just happens to be on the corner. Bottom line question is why can't I just cross wherever the hell I want to? It's because like most things in life, stuff that comes easy is either wrong or generally not worth the effort. After all the years of infidelity and after all the years of people getting caught partaking in the act of infidelity, it shocks me – no it astounds me that there at not thousands of books on how to successfully circumvent this topic. If you think about it, car accidents occur all the time – yet there are countless books available on safe and effective driving. There are even a number of books on defensive driving. Bad sex abounds between certain couples even though there are a multitude of books on what to do to make it better. The topic of catching someone cheating is of particular interest to many but the other hand, teaching someone how to cheat, seems to be only on the minds of the perverted. Ain't that something? Infidelity is one of the biggest causes of break ups today and why, because few people give it any importance. Don't misunderstand me; people do pay attention to infidelity when it's up close and personal but the majority of the time they use the 'ignore it and it'll go away' strategy. One would think, especially one with common sense, that in order to be the best at something or at least an adequate contender, he or she would need to have a complete understanding of everything said activity entails. However, certain people in their infinite wisdom are still hoping and wishing that lady luck will supersede proper planning and skill. Please understand that no amount of luck, as well as no amount of skill will always dictate the winner of the infidelity competition but as history has almost always shown, a little planning is better than none at all. When someone chooses to ignore rules and advice put in place to help them and perhaps better his or her life, dire or at least unpleasant consequences are sure to follow. A prime example would be driving. If someone were to drive a car for the first time without even a basic understanding of traffic laws or without knowing the effort necessary to control a moving vehicle, accidents would be sure to follow. The same thing goes with sex. Some people still believe that sexual intercourse only consists of a man making the movements while a woman lies there and either enjoys it, fakes it or complains. Now granted, a book will not automatically turn bad sex into good but bad sex is like bad cooking; it will never get better if you continue to do the same thing. The bottom line is the more you know, the better off you will likely be. Knowing what to do before committing an indiscretion will almost always lower an individual's chances of getting caught. The problem is, aside from not giving indiscretions like infidelity the respect, which is due; people don't always know what to do to successfully commit those indiscretions in the first place. When it comes to successful infidelity, discretion and deception are the two biggest necessities for success. By 'successful' infidelity, I mean an adulterous liaison where nobody gets caught or at least not caught in the traditional sense. Many times people are aware of the trifling games their significant other happens to be playing; yet they say nothing. These two ingredients, deception & discretion, work best in conjunction with one another even though they are more than sufficient alone. As mentioned in several of my prior publications, there is no limit to the density of deception in this world. Deception can stem from birth in some cases and depending upon the level of discretion, that deception can last a lifetime. The fact that certain types of deception are rarely questioned, for instance the 'I'm pregnant and it's your baby' is what adds to deception's longevity. If a man is involved with a woman in a supposedly happy relationship and the woman turns up pregnant and the man does not believe her, then either he is 'no good' in every sense of the word or his significant other is just as bad. An issue of this nature would usually only come about if a prior act of infidelity or deception has either occurred or been highly suspected of occurring. An effective method of committing infidelity, which entails both discretion and deception, is that of using numbers to signify a person's location. Often what people who are involved in an adulterous relationship will do when planning to meet is call each other and divulge the exact locale of their future rendezvous. What these people do not take into account is the possibility that their communication devices may be tapped. Phone calls can be easily recorded. Computer keystrokes can be copied remotely and incriminating emails, which were thought to be previously deleted, can be retrieved. The process of quickly undoing what has been done to avoid getting caught is a good one but it pales in comparison to adequate and well thought out planning. That process pales in comparison even more to not doing bad at all. For the longest of time, people have maintained this belief that their significant others are not as smart as they themselves are – especially when it comes to the field of infidelity. This invincible feeling is what causes many to lose happiness, families and sometimes lives. In the case above with people using the telephone to set up a meeting, too often the conversation will go as follows:

'She won't be home for hours'

'Okay, so do you want me to come over to your house?'

'No, too much cleaning up afterwards'

'Okay so what do I do?'

'Meet me on Main Street, in front of the jewelry store with the red awning at 3:00.'

Now if this conversation were being had by a couple in close proximity to one another, where no one else could see or hear them, then it would be perfectly fine. However as I tell people all the time, big brother is always watching and so is big sister, big husband and big wife. Let's say the husband in the above example had the above conversation with his mistress, not knowing the wife had installed a telephone conversation recorder inside the handset of the phone. It goes without saying; the husband would be in a pretty bad situation, especially if the wife is of a violent nature. Remember I never advocate cheating but if I did, it would be at the top of my suggestion list for the husband to use a particular number to conceal the meeting place. Using the above example, the husband and the mistress could have had the same conversation, only not as incriminating and instead of ending with let's meet on main street at 3:00, could have simply said 'I'll meet you at one.' The word 'one' can encompass so many things that if someone were actually listening or had planted a recording device, they would be totally in a fog as to the location, especially if one o'clock rolls around and the husband is still sitting at home in his drawers. If the husband and his mistress were smart, they would have devised a plan way in advance to counteract any potential problems, which may occur. The number one could be used to mean 'meet me at Main Street at 8:30pm.' Now someone who is not hip to this kind of trickery will think that probably the husband either forgot about the one o'clock meeting or was trying to brush off who ever was on the line, especially if one o'clock passes and the husband goes nowhere. This belief could be solidified even further if the husband invites the wife somewhere entirely different at one p.m. say for instance to meet a female co – worker and pick up some office related materials. If the wife did somehow overhear the conversation and the husband dispels the wife's belief that he is doing something wrong, especially in the manner described above, then the husband is home free. If you plan to employ a technique such as this, a good idea would be to use more than one number, for instance – 'one' means meet me at Main Street, 'two' means meet me on Trinity Avenue and bring some alcohol. This process can also be changed to include actual places which stand for other places, for instance if you were to say 'meet me on Main Street' the other party would instantly know that Main Street is a code phrase for meet me on Taylor Ave.

I have to go back to The Correct Way To Fool Around part one for a second because it seems that people have forgotten the most basic of rules when it comes to infidelity. If you do not want your indiscretions to be known, simply don't tell anyone. This does not mean don't get on national television and say 'hey I had sex with you know who' it simply means don't give out that tiny bit of information that you think is harmless but will eventually lead to your infidelity's discovery and quite possibly your demise. What a lot of people don't realize is that there are a lot of jealous mothers out here. These jmf's consist of best friends, who sometimes can be your worst moral enemy, family members who think that they should have been involved with the person you are involved with and complete strangers who know you or your adulterous situation from a far. People think that as long as they don't mention the word sex when talking about their involvement with another, then whomever they are talking to will not be smart enough or clever enough to figure out that sex is actually part of the equation. Sometimes the information you give out maybe as insignificant as letting your natural partner know you run a successful home based business. You may be under the impression, as most, that he or she will not tell anyone or if they do tell someone, whoever they tell will only be interested in helping further your career. But it doesn't happen like that. Your natural partner, who you think only associates with clean cut, nice, positive attitude people because he or she embodies those attributes himself, happens to have a friend of a friend or a friend of a cousin who likes you and with whom you regularly converse. This friend is nothing like the natural partner. This friend is abrasive and violent to everybody, except her. Your natural partner tells this friend, that the two of them cannot be together on an intimate level because there is someone else. You are that someone else. Your natural partner, in one of her platonic phone conversations, tells the friend of a friend about your successful business and this friend becomes interested. He wants to meet you. Now this is a big world, some will say massive but when it comes to certain situations, this world is unbelievably small. Let's say this friend of a friend of your natural partner just happens to know the person you are in a relationship with. This person may have been interested in your significant other for the longest but realized that since the two of you were married and your significant other respected those vows publicly and repetitively, this person backed off. Imagine the surprise when this friend of a friend of your natural partner's realizes that he couldn't get any play from your natural partner because you were cheating on your wife with her. Now you may not know that this person was interested in your wife at all but he will have more than ample opportunity to devise a plan in which to blackmail you into a number of things. This person can go and let your wife know about your affair, that way bettering his chances with her or he can let your natural partner know that you are in fact married, if you didn't already tell her, thereby messing up things with you and your natural partner and consequently bettering his chances with her as well. Now obviously, if you are in a natural relationship and you have half an ounce of common sense or maybe you haven't any common sense at all but you have read my first book, The Correct

Way To Fool Around, then chances are you know to keep your mouth shut at all costs. One of the biggest problems however with perpetrating a successful affair is the task of conveying this idea to your natural partner. Everybody has a tell all outlet. This outlet can be a diary, a journal, a best friend or even a chat line. These are your enemies. People can be broken. Diaries can be broken into. Chat lines are the worst of all because given the fact that the possibility of complete anonymity is there, you may never know exactly whom you are conversing with and what's even worse, you may be conversing with somebody who knows your significant other. The more outlets there are, the more chance a leak can be formed. If you and your natural partner are the only two who are aware of the indiscretion, chances are your indiscretion will continue for as long as possible. People have a habit of only believing what they see and this is mainly because many people, not all but many in this world are ignorant. This is one of the reasons many people do not believe in a higher power. I'm not trying to turn this into a religious lesson but faith is required in most religions because the idea of a higher power cannot be seen. If the majority of people in this world do not see you cheating, they will assume that you don't. If that same group of people does not see you with a member of the opposite sex in a manner, which is consistent with people involved in a relationship, more than likely, they will assume you are homosexual. Again, nothing but ignorance. This can be used to your advantage by keeping your activities hidden and your mouth shut. Let people think what they will. Nine times out of ten, if they are so busy concerning themselves with what is going on in your life, there is probably very little going on in theirs. When people lie, far too often they say things that they themselves would not believe if they were being told to them. What people need to do is make a lie believable to the person they are telling the lie to. For instance, let's take those pesky ass telemarketers or those street solicitors who always have some scam or option to get your money. It used to be when you were approached and you didn't feel like giving them the time of day as well as your money, you could simply say I only have credit cards. That would usually end the conversation but as of late, these people have quickly moved up the tech ladder, carrying credit card machines in those handy dandy little pouches, with which they can take your information any place, any time. I found this out first hand because I tried the 'I only have a credit card line' and the son of a bitch pulled the machine out of his bag and said MasterCard or Visa. I was about to walk away but I had already committed myself by telling him I was interested in helping the poor unfortunate children of some third world country and just up and leaving after letting him know I had the means to help would have made me look more of hypocrite than some of our in office politicians. So I paid but I learned a valuable lesson in the process. Instead of lying and hoping the person I was lying to had no means to counter my argument, I began to lie but not before eliminating every possible counter measure the person I was lying to could have. I did have the opportunity to be approached by another bleeding heart, child sponsor solicitor and instead of telling him I had no cash or just credit cards, I told him how much I wanted to help but at the present time I was between jobs and as of January 1, I cut up my credit cards so as not to cement myself any further in inescapable debt. The only thing the poor guy could do was sympathize and offer to send me to the so called organization's website. I told him I would visit as I walked away, laughing my ass off, knowing I had no intention whatsoever of entertaining the thought of him or his solicitation effort ever again. Now there are other ways this situation could have been handled, for instance saying I had no cash - but what these people have a habit of doing is concentrating their efforts in high traffic areas, like shopping centers or districts. If a person is walking through a shopping district, the assumption will be that that person has money, even if he doesn't. Now to tell a solicitor that you are broke is about the same as saying I don't want to help your nasty, crusty ass. Now while this is probably true, you want to make him look like the bad guy for inconveniencing you, not the other way around. If you just say you don't have any cash, they will pretty much assume you're lying. Lying is almost always a viable option to get out of unpleasant situations but it's more about how you do it, rather than the fact that you do it. This is why, when in a relationship, communication is essential. You must find out all you can about how a person feels about certain things so that you can more easily manipulate that individual if and when you decide to cheat. The reason January 1 is such an important date is because that is the time of year the majority of the people in this world make those impossible to keep resolutions, least of which, the one about getting out of debt. Everybody knows people make weight loss resolutions, better job resolutions and a boatload of others. The point here is if you use something, which has an enormous following or at least a decent number of people who have done it before you, your lie will have a better chance at being believed.

    One of the really big things, which will get a prospective cheater in trouble, is not realizing that this world is not perfect. Too often, people will assume that traffic is always predictable, bus and train service is always reliable and power failures only occur once every fifteen years. Most people, especially those who live in big cities should know the above is not true. Life is unpredictable. Cheaters often get caught because they do not keep up with current events. These current events need not be about the world at large as much as an individual's community. For instance, a person could have an ongoing affair with someone for months. The affair could be perpetrated by this person pretending to go to work everyday, when in actuality; he or she is going to the home of the jezebel or jody. Let's say also for instance, there were to be a city wide black out, which lasts for the majority of the day. If the person who is cheating spends all day screwing, chances are pretty certain he or she will be unaware of this fact. Then what will subsequently happen is this person will go home and the significant other will ask something to the effect of 'how'd you get home?' the cheating partner, who has no idea of the black out may say the usual response – to wit 'I took the train or bus.' At this time, the innocent party will have every right to lose his or her fucking mind because he or she has just caught the other in a lie. Now while many affairs occur many miles away the home (which if you are planning to have one is the smart thing) many more occur in the general vicinity of the perpetrator's residence. If only the above exampled individual had turned on a television and found out what was going on in the world, he or she might still have a place to sleep.

When it comes to infidelity, the simplest overlooked measures are what get people caught all the time. I once had a friend tell me about one of the ways he got busted and it started me thinking. He mentioned how he would pick his girlfriend up every day almost immediately after he dropped his wife off at work. It doesn't take a brain surgeon to figure out what they were doing during the eight hours the wife was at work – they were fucking. Most of the time the infidelity (according to him) took place at locations other than the home and away from places that either of them usually frequent. He never drove to his wife's job without taking a shower and he always washed his clothes, dried them and put them back on to make sure that there was no possible trace of another woman's scent anywhere on him. He even took his car to the car wash to have it cleaned inside and out each day he and his mistress had their liaisons. It seemed like this man had every base covered, as should be the case when a person partakes in the act of infidelity. Unfortunately, there was one simple thing he forgot to do. His wife, it had come to be known, purchased a thirty dollar, voice activated recorder and placed it inside the pouch behind the driver's side seat. Now even though this adulterous couple had never actually had sex inside the car, the fact that their meetings and conversations were caught and recorded provided more than enough evidence for the wife. Now I will be the last one to suggest that my friend should have done a door to door car search before picking up his mistress because almost nobody will believe that their significant will be so sneaky – especially if the party committing the indiscretion is otherwise careful. What I would suggest however is that whatever conversations the couple have or plan to have be void of any reference to the planned affair. That way if and when the wife reviews the recording device, it will seem as if the interaction between the husband and the mistress is purely platonic. This is one of the hardest things to do because whenever people have a sexual relationship, there are feelings involved. The parties may be able to temporarily downplay or put aside those feelings but they will be there. Unless the relationship is between a prostitute and her 'john' chances are there will be conversations and at least one of those conversations will revolve around the sex act. What a couple needs to do if they want to alleviate the possibility of capture is talk about everything except the rendezvous. This includes the husband talking to the mistress about how much he loves his wife and what presents he is planning to buy her, even if this is total bull. This also includes the mistress, if she is single, asking the husband to play matchmaker for her – anything to divert attention away from the truth. To commit successful infidelity, one must always believe that the significant other is always hot on the cheating parties trail. This belief is what will cause the cheating party to be not one but two and maybe even three steps ahead of the suspicious significant other. It may seem as if the cheaters are being paranoid but paranoia has long been equated rather confused with extreme concern. When a person is extremely concerned about something, it is very unlikely that that person will do anything less than pay attention to every detail possible. A person that is suspicious of their significant other will try almost anything in his or her power to dispel the belief that he or she is cheating. This includes following, questioning, badgering, even resorting to the methods of 007 as stated above. A person that is cheating on his or her significant other needs to be just as diligent in blocking the efforts of the significant other's pursuits. This includes allowing one's self to be followed, allowing one's self to be questioned and badgered and even <u>sometimes</u> doing a backseat, voice activated recorder search. Nobody knows to what extent a person who is suspicious of their significant other will go to prove their fidelity. Remember if you are cheating and your significant other does not seem to care about your activities – even in the least, then that should be a clear cut sign for you to be extra diligent when covering your tracks. Remember also that deception works both ways; on the part of the cheater so that the infidelity will not be exposed and on the part of the innocent party in an attempt to expose it. In The Correct Way

To Fool Around part one, I suggested that a person should never lie about being with a member of the opposite sex. Doing this is almost a guaranteed method to getting caught or if not caught, then very much suspected of having an affair. Instead a person should – if necessary, lie about why he or she was with that particular person. If for instance my friend had employed this technique, the wife would have had no real way of knowing whether her husband was telling the truth or whether it was a well thought out plan to successfully combat the possibility of him getting caught. If my friend who shall continue to be nameless, had said something to the effect of 'honey I have to pick up Tasha after I drop you off at work and take her to wherever' the wife may have been inquisitive, she may have been doubtful of the husband's story, she may have even been mad as all hell - but as long as the foundation was adequately laid, what could she really say? Unless the wife had to deal with a prior bout of infidelity involving Tasha or some other woman and as a result she gave her husband specific instructions regarding having any women in his car, she really would have little reason to get mad or suspicious. Any number of people could have come to her, called her or emailed her the information that they saw her husband driving around another girl. It would not likely perturb the wife nearly as much as it would if she had not known in advance. A simple move such as this would probably have saved my friend his six year relationship. Now I would expect nothing less than a woman being pissed off as hell if she catches her man cheating but I would not always expect the relationship to end. I would expect the silent treatment, I would expect the separation, I would even expect the retaliation but to end a relationship because of one infraction, that strikes me as just a little extreme. Now granted, infidelity is a big infraction, maybe even the biggest relationship infraction there is but does that mean that once the bond of fidelity is broken there is never any chance at retribution or reconciliation? I think not. In the case of my friend, I always tell him 'it wasn't the infidelity, which caused the breakup. The infidelity was the straw that broke the camel's back.' People cannot be in a relationship for six years and not have problems. On the same note people cannot be in love and not be willing to at least attempt to work out some of the problems they do have. Since my friend's wife left him soon after the recorder was found, it was clearly evident that she needed or wanted an out. Again the infidelity was the culmination of six years of unresolved problems. This was her out. I know many people are probably going to disagree with me but I believe that if a couple who is truly in love has to deal with a one time affair, there is often a strong chance that that couple can pick up and move on. The operative words here being 'in love.' People make mistakes – always have –

always will. If a person cheats one time and there is a sufficient amount of love in the relationship, forgiveness can enter and heal the wound. I find it exceptionally hard to believe that a couple can build a relationship, build a family and a future and have it toppled by one act of infidelity. In situations such as this a person must wonder; how much love if any was actually there? You see just like it takes sometimes years and years to build on the foundation of love, it should take at least that long for it to break apart. If on the other hand a couple has had to deal with a recurring affair or many different affairs, then I believe the relationship is more than over. One affair most will agree is forgivable because as mentioned before everybody makes mistakes – but when a person does not learn from said mistake, that person is almost certainly destined to repeat it. When a person cheats and continues to cheat, he or she 1) has a problem 2) is looking for help with the problem and 3) believes that cheating is somehow actually solving the problem, which is causing him or her to cheat in the first place.

Let's talk about some of the new technology in this world for a second. Technology is a wonderful thing. It is so wonderful that there are almost not enough words to explain how wonderful it actually is. When it comes to committing infidelity, utilizing the latest gadgets makes communicating an absolute breeze. A few years ago, there was no such thing as texting, yet now everybody and their mother is typing away at breakneck speeds everywhere you look. This is a wonderful thing for some people who commit infidelity because these people can be engaged in an intimate conversation with the person they are cheating with in the immediate presence of their significant other without the significant other having any idea what the other person is doing. Now imagine for a second if there were no such thing as texting. The person cheating would have to speak softly so as not to arouse suspicion or speak in code (pretending he or she is talking to a member of the same sex) or not take the call until the significant other is nowhere around. Texting eliminates the need for the previous options because it makes communication virtually impossible to detect unless somebody is literally looking over that person's shoulder. If someone were to question a person, who is texting a love interest, about what that person was actually doing, that person could make up any number of excuses – from playing a game to jotting down appointment details. And depending upon how fast that person was able to switch applications on the device he or she was using, chances are that person would never get caught. It's almost the same as when a person is checking his personal email on the company's time as well as on the company's computer and the boss happens to walk by, the person can minimize the screen to reflect the spreadsheet or whatever the person's job entails until the boss walks on by. Like I mentioned before, this is a wonderful thing. But as with every good thing in this world, I believe there is an opposite and equal bad. Technology, as good as it is, is many times flawed. There are often bugs, which have to be worked out with new and existing programs and gadgets. One of those flaws is what many phones do when they are placed inside of a pocket. These phones place calls by themselves. I guess this gives new meaning to the term 'smart phones.' Now I do not mean that these phones will completely dial someone's number by themselves but if they are placed in a pocket or somewhere where there is enough friction or contact, the phone may actually redial the last number called or worst case scenario, may find its way into the phonebook and dial anybody's number. I had experienced this firsthand by my girlfriend or should I say ex girlfriend not realizing that her phone was still on after she disconnected from me. The phone kept recording her conversation for a good five to seven minutes after we'd initially hung up. I found this out because when I said hello, nobody answered but I heard her voice. So what did I do? I did what every other insecure, jealous, tired of the relationship I was in and wanted a way out but had none, person would do. I listened. I heard her talking to another fella about how she had to make a daily 'let him know I care' call so I wouldn't suspect that she was cheating (or as she put it 'doing her thing.' I came to find out that she and the dude she was talking to worked together – as I also came to find out that her job was infidelity central – meaning everybody was cheating on their significant others. The conversation I overheard included (and I quote) 'so when you gonna give me some more of that dick?' and 'he works a double shift on Saturdays so we can get together then.' I thought that she couldn't be so fucking careless and blatant in her activities and that she called me with the express intent of letting me hear the phone conversation because she was sick of me and wanted a way out of the relationship. This was until I used her cell phone and had the same thing happen. I pressed the end call button after my conversation was over but the line was still active. This is why cheaters need to be especially careful. You can get caught by unintentionally giving your mate the information he or she desires. As for me and her, we didn't break up immediately after that incident because the sex was great, I'm not gonna lie to you but what really broke the camel's back was the fact that she tried to turn around her insecurities and indiscretions and place them on me. She began to accuse me without provocation, <u>which is what cheaters often do</u> and she would lie about going out with this dude by saying she was having a 'girls night out' type of thing. I knew she was lying because after the phone incident, my curiosity was peaked and I began to follow her. Maybe the following thing was wrong on my part but like I have said a million times before, the power of the conscience is very strong especially if the conscience is not clear. Oh by the way, the following did pay off. I did observe her with one of her girlfriends and a couple of gentlemen. Funny how when I called her during her 'girls night out' she mentioned that she was with one of her female friends but totally neglected to mention anything about the two dudes. When she arrived home, she didn't mention anything about them then either. Guess it wasn't that important or maybe it was because she had so much fun that she thought I would be jealous and she didn't tell me because she wanted to spare my feelings…how thoughtful. Getting back to the phones, let's think about the possible ramifications of this for a second. I mentioned previously how if a phone is jostled around in a pocket or pocketbook, it may go through a myriad of functions, up to and including dialing someone in the phonebook or someone totally new. What if a couple were having turmoil in their relationship because of prior infidelity or even because of the thought of unproven infidelity and a hang up call was received at this individual's home? Let's say the woman in the relationship was so insecure or unbelieving of her husband that she called the number back and some other female picked up the phone. If this woman asks 'did you just call my house and the person who owns the cell phone says no (which is the truth) she will be thought of as a liar, number one and number two, the husband who may or may not be innocent will be thought of as screwing this woman or if not screwing her, then having knowledge of her. This is where trust would usually come in and save the day but as most everyone in a relationship knows trust is usually only contingent upon good times and as long as there were no prior bouts of infidelity or trust destroying situations.

Continuing with technology, in The Correct Way To Fool Around part 2, I mentioned a much overlooked method of entrapment called the spoof card. This is basically something, which will allow one caller to have virtually any other phone number appear on someone's caller id. I used to use this card to piss people off just because I'm that type of guy but think of how this invention can cause trouble in a relationship. Let's say someone in a relationship was busted cheating at some point and the significant other decided that the love was greater than the indiscretion and they stayed together. Let's also say that someone outside of the relationship who was aware of the indiscretion and who knew all of the parties involved, felt that he or she could be a better partner to the one who was the innocent party in the previous affair. This person could continually make it seem as if the person involved in the affair is still calling either the home or the cell of the married or committed individual. There will have to be a level of trust, which is almost unheard of to be able to get past this situation if the parties involved do not know of the methods of entrapment available – especially the one above. It's ashamed but people fear change and they don't just fear it, they are petrified of it. Technology always changes and those who fear it or who are petrified of it will unfortunately become victims of it.

One final note I feel I need to reiterate before I end this chapter. People have to realize that there are others who make a habit, career or science out of following the activities or exploits of others. For this reason alone, people who cheat need to be extra diligent when covering their tracks. This includes the deletion of all possible evidence. One of the ways many tech savvy folks get caught is by hitting the delete button on their computers after having a steamy conversation via email or instant messenger. They get caught because they think that this is all that is necessary to eradicate the evidence of the conversation. These people don't realize that computers still save information even after it is deleted – and all which is necessary to retrieve it is a few strokes of the history button or if not that, then there always is the undo delete trash button. How do you think law enforcement always seems to have the uncanny ability to pull up damaging information, which was believed to be previously deleted? Of course they have computer experts whose sole purpose in life is to recover evidence, which will help put the perpetrator in jail. Now granted you, as the average cheater, may not have the technical skills necessary to either lock the computer in such a way that will prevent almost anybody from accessing it or deleting the damaging information so far that it will take one of those law enforcement geeks months to find it but you can take a few simple precautions. The best advice I can give is to always permanently delete anything from your computer that you would not want your significant other to find. Make sure you check the hard drive and if you inadvertently saved whatever information you didn't mean to, make sure you delete it from the hard drive. What's funny is how many people don't think about anything unless it's right in front of their faces and in black and white. If they don't see anything on the screen often they will assume that whatever was there has been completely erased and these people are free to continuing doing whatever it was they were doing before. Good luck with that. Another thing I can advise is if you are a person who suffers from 'oops, I forgot what I did five minutes ago' then you should always use an Internet café to commit your online indiscretions. You should not only not use the same computer inside a particular location; you should not or never use the same location. When a person does the same thing, over and over, that person begins to have a following or if not a following, then followers. These are people who notice you either going into the Internet café day after day or coming out of the Internet café day after day or who work at the Internet café day after day. If the affair you are involved in for whatever reason goes wrong, and you have to quickly extricate yourself from any type of connection to that person, imagine how easy it would be to implicate yourself if people came around asking questions to the effect of 'ever seen this guy before.' Imagine also if for whatever reason, there was the need to retrieve your online conversation. If people know you and know which computer you sit at, it would not be as hard as it would if they didn't. If every time you wanted to communicate with your sweetie and you used a different location, the powers that be would have to tail you to positively identify those locations. That of course leaves the problem of someone already knowing your email and im addresses and screen names but just as there are already millions of screen names and possibly as many email accounts, there is also the possibility of you and your sweetie having more than one of each and switching them up as necessary.

One other thing many people forget to do is alter the phone logs after they finish a call. This is relatively simple. All a person has to do is erase either the calls made or the calls received. What some people do is hold conversations with the one they are cheating with, hang up and then leave the phone laying around – prime opportunity for the significant other to find it. This is a rookie mistake. C Y A (covering your ass) should always be your first priority. When it comes to phone records many people will delete only the call that they do not want the significant other to see. This is good but what should be done is the deletion of all of the numbers in the list because if your significant other happens to notice you on the phone and then asks to see your phone when you finish the call and you are dumb enough to give it to him or her, he or she will be livid or at least highly suspicious if they see that you erased the last call. If however you were to erase all of the numbers and the significant other asks to see your phone, you can make up a myriad of excuses as to why the entire list is empty. If you have a touch screen phone like I do you can always say something to the effect of 'I accidentally touched the wrong part of the screen and inadvertently deleted the numbers.' Of course there will be doubt with this story but think about something; who hasn't experienced a cell phone dialing a number by itself because the keypad wasn't locked or the phone continuing to record someone's conversation because it wasn't properly shut off? Point I'm trying to make is people make mistakes and technology fails. A person needs to use these things to his or her advantage if he or she wants to be able to not get caught.

Chapter Three
The Correct Way To Fool Around

The Correct Way To Fool Around is more than just the controversial title of a series of very popular books. I believe it is a thought process. It is an attitude, which must be undertaken to successfully commit as well as detect the act of infidelity. For a person to fool around, he or she must be void of certain feelings, such as loyalty, honesty and last but not least, commitment. Granted, commitment is not a feeling. It is however something, which must be included when one speaks of relationship necessities. The person committing or contemplating infidelity must be one who is willing to risk family, health, finances and stability for pleasure. Infidelity by most accounts is wrong. There are some religions and some people in general who believe it is okay but these factions have serious moral dilemmas, with which to deal. As mentioned before, the correct way to fool around is a thought process. It is a process, which entails being the best at what one does. It involves study, it involves practice and it involves concentration. To drive a car, one cannot simply get in and drive. (They can but chances are they will not do it very well). There are lessons, which have to be learned and mistakes, which have to be made. To be proficient at any type of employment, one must possess at least a basic level of understanding of what said job entails. This is much the overlooked philosophy behind cheating. A conservative estimate would be that most of the people in this world who commit infidelity do it either because of the 'caught' ideology. They are either 'caught' up in the moment or they just don't think they are going to get 'caught.' Getting caught up in the moment is understandable because few people actually plan to commit adultery – especially those who are normally faithful. Those who don't think they are going to get caught are the ones who end up in divorces, bankruptcies and murder/suicides. The reason between the differences is that those who get caught up in the moment usually get caught up that one particular time and those who think they won't get caught continue to get caught up, time and time again. As life continues to show, the more a person does something, the more recognition that person will receive. If a person plays basketball at the same gym everyday, he will be noticed. If a person plays basketball at that same gym everyday and becomes exceedingly proficient at the sport, he will be noticed even more. On the opposite end of the spectrum, if that person were to involve himself in a particular negative activity, the chance he has to get noticed or caught in that particular negative activity will mirror the amount of times he does the negative activity. The idea behind The Correct Way To Fool Around is more than just not getting caught. It is also knowing what a cheater does to not get caught so that a person can be one step ahead of the game. Infidelity has to be studied and not just from the perspective of what it is and why it is but also how it is done. Infidelity must also be analyzed from the perspective of the victim and the perpetrator. Once mastery of each angle or perspective is completed, then and only then can one say he or she has a pretty good idea of how to fool around correctly.

What follows are three examples of infidelity and how they can be perpetrated as well as exposed.

1) A married couple has a young child. They both work full time, while the nineteen year old babysitter who makes ten bucks an hour visits the home each day to take care of the child. The wife works at night and the husband works during the day. One day the husband offers the teenage babysitter the opportunity to make a few hundred extra dollars by performing wifely duties that the wife is not able to due to her schedule. The babysitter accepts and she and the husband take childcare to a whole new level.
2) A married couple both work full time at the same organization. They have no kids. The wife is sleeping with the boss of the company. The husband has no idea of the affair but the bosses' wife does.
3) A man and woman are dating. There is no promise of commitment but the belief of exclusivity is there. This

couple does not live together nor do they share any children. One female, outside of the relationship, who is aware that the couple has certain feelings for each other, desires a relationship with the man. The man, his loose morals, his promiscuous nature and the girl hook up. It is only a one time thing and the girlfriend never finds out.

In example number one, the husband is probably thinking that he has gotten away or is getting away scot free with infidelity because his wife has yet to approach him with any accusations. However what he does not know is that the wife has, without his knowledge, installed a nanny cam to keep watch on the babysitter. Imagine her surprise! What the husband could and should have done is meet the babysitter on her day off, away from the home to minimize his chances of getting caught. What would have been an even wiser decision would have been for the husband to fool around with someone totally different. Understanding The Correct Way To Fool Around would let a person know that there are underlying or unresolved issues in the relationship, which would make the husband become interested in the babysitter in the first place. One of those possible issues could have been the fact the husband desires a certain type of female, particularly one who is young, in shape and with little body fat – pretty much the way most teenagers are. The wife, as good to the husband as she probably is, could not be in shape or as in shape as much as the husband likes. She is most likely older and possibly carries a few extra pounds from the baby's arrival or from the fact that she has a good paying job and rewards herself by sampling any and every type of new food she can get her hands on. The wife could have been what the husband desired at one time but now for whatever reason the husband's interests lie elsewhere. People have to realize something; when there is something or someone that a person has or has a connection to and it is taken away – even for a little while, when something or someone, which resembles what was taken away comes into the equation, of course there will be an attraction to it or a longing for it. Now I'm not saying that it is in any way right to act on the attraction, I'm just saying that the attraction will more than likely be there. One of the many mistaken beliefs people have (especially women) is this one about 'if you loved me at one hundred and thirty pounds, then you should still love me at two hundred and thirty pounds.' People don't always do that. It does not mean that the person who is involved with the weight gainer is shallow - it can just mean the he or she desires a certain thing and if by chance that certain thing which he or she desires just happens to be taken away, the desire for it will still be there. I am not in any way making excuses for the father propositioning the babysitter, I'm just trying to have people understand that there will always be certain desires in people's lives which may never disappear.

In example number two, the infidelity is easily committed because the married woman and her boss are basically 'hiding in plain sight' with their indiscretion. As with many jobs, when relatives work together, they are often placed in different departments so as not to create personal conflict during working hours. The same holds true for married people. It is a very well known fact that married folks have a greater tendency to argue and bring their home problems to the 9 – 5. To circumvent this at the workplace, companies will usually keep the married couples as far away from each other if they employ them at all. Now using this company philosophy, the boss of the company can at any time, call the married woman to his office under the guise of employment related business. The husband would more than likely never question or accuse the boss simply for fear of employment related repercussions. This leaves the husband at a severe disadvantage because if at any time he makes an accusation against his boss, all the boss would have to do is dare him to prove it. If the wife does not complain, the boss' defense could be that any interaction between him and the accusers wife is strictly business related – and if there is nothing to disprove the boss' alibi, what can the husband say? If the boss' wife on the other hand knows what is going on between the two, she is in a position of power herself because she can easily break up the marriage between the mistress and her husband by simply telling the husband of the wife that the boss is sleeping with. As far as repercussions go, the boss really won't have much to fear since 1) he is the boss, so his job is pretty safe unless he is using his power and position to coerce the woman into in affair and if that is the case then there are many things the woman can do regarding sexual harassment. 2) If he is so blatant or careless as to let his wife find out, chances are he does not give enough of a damn to care about it either way.

In example number three, the man has basically done what almost every other committed man in existence has either done or thought of at least once. He has stolen some booty! The man is in a very good position right now. He and his girlfriend are dating but not married. The affair 'if you can call it that' ended quickly and successfully – meaning nobody was hurt or caught and both achieved that ever elusive orgasm. Due to the fact that the couple was not married or engaged, the infidelity could be explained as nothing more than the man exploring options to see if he really desires commitment. Of course if the girlfriend were to ever find out she would most likely be understandably pissed. However, guys have this thing we do, which often helps us escape from many relationship ramifications. It's called the one last time defense. This is what is used in boyfriend and girlfriend relationships when a dude gets caught. The defense goes as follows 'baby, I didn't mean to cheat, it meant nothing! It was just a one last thing before I proposed to you.' I know 99% of the women reading this are probably saying yea right – that's some bullshit! But what the actual bullshit is – is just how many of you women fall for that exact line. Guys are historically and infamously known for having bachelor parties. If a man comes at an otherwise smart woman with this 'bachelor party inspired' bullshit, chances are many women will let the fact that the man is planning to propose supersede the fact that the woman has actually caught him cheating. And we all know what happens next, nine times out of ten the woman forgives him and makes the boyfriend say those infamous nine words 'now you promise that was the last time, right?' Followed by those other infamous words 'You won't do it again, right?' to which the man will gleefully answer 'I promise dear, I will never do it again.' (All the while having his fingers mentally crossed behind his back!) This of course leads to the fake engagement ring – Understand the ring may be real but the sentiment behind it will more than likely be fake. Then what follows is the never ending engagement where the man is free to screw as many 'one last time' women as he possibly can. It will be easy because his girlfriend has a ring and as history has many times shown, just like kryptonite makes superman powerless, a ring often makes a woman senseless. She will assume that EVENTUALLY she will get married – no matter how many years eventually actually takes. So even if the woman with the ring and the cheating boyfriend do finally get married, it will more than likely be long after he has finished cheating. The woman outside of the relationship who just wanted to have a fling with the involved man seems to be the only one who makes out well in this situation because chances are she will still be free to screw whoever whenever she wants. She will make out well because she has nobody to answer to and if she was to ever be questioned by the wife of the man she is cheating with, all she would have to say is 'He told me he was single.' A note to everybody reading this; this situation cannot be completely avoided; it can only be substantially alleviated. People are going to do what they are going to do and nothing short of an act of God or they themselves changing their plans to do whatever it is they were going to do in the first place will stop them. The way situations such as this and many others can be substantially alleviated is through constant and thorough communication. What people still in the year of 2010 don't do or don't like to do very much is communicate their feelings. They will be intrigued by the thought of infidelity. They will be pressured by the possibility of infidelity. They may even be imprisoned by the thought that their significant other is indulging in the act of infidelity but nine times out of ten, these people will not communicate these feelings to one another. This is how infidelity spreads. It does not spread by a person being a sex maniac. It does not spread by there not being an ample amount of sex being had in the relationship. It spreads by either no communication or the wrong type of communication. Now I know plenty of you are wondering what could possibly be the wrong type of communication, I mean after all talking is talking, isn't it? True, talking is talking but you can talk to a person as well as at a person. To is highly preferred. Communication can be verbal as well as non verbal as well as wrong. The wrong type of communication is 'honey, how was work today? Did anybody aggravate you at the office? Aunt Zelda from Poughkeepsie is coming to spend a couple of weeks with us.' This is communicating, it is verbal but it is general and far too often recurring. Some couples say the same thing day after day, week after week, year after year – like hi honey, how was your day? Did anybody aggravate you at the office?' This type of communication is wrong because it does not focus on specifics, like 'honey, I'm not feeling fulfilled in this relationship' or 'honey, there's someone in the office who likes me and who for some reason or other I've been attracted to – let's talk.' Far too often honest communication is met with cynicism and hostility like 'oh you think this motherfucker is attractive, then why don't you go fuck him?' For communication to work it has to be open; it has to be mutual and it has to be ongoing. People aren't honest with their feelings in relationships for many reasons but many times they aren't allowed to be honest with their partners either. Sometimes the partners refuse to accept that the relationship is not 100%. These people feel that a relationship <u>has</u> to work at all costs. They can do this by bullying, refusing to leave or by a myriad of other methods. This can come from family history or from the fact that some people are just crazy. To put it simply, the correct way to fool around is about being open enough to talk about feelings, thoughts and desires, which would drive a person toward infidelity in the first place. It is not solely about teaching infidelity committing tactics; it is about teaching awareness. It's sad but true, many people are not aware of what is actually going on in their relationships. They want to believe they are. They even tell their friends they are but if that were actually the case, would infidelity be as easily able to infect as many relationships as it has and still continues to do? I think not. This is the same thing as with these delusional parents who believe their children are actually above doing wrong. No one is immune from bad habits, especially kids, just like no relationship is immune from infidelity. People need to talk more, communicate more, interact with each other more so that infidelity can be exposed and quite possibly stopped in its tracks. Remember a talk about infidelity will rarely last. Communicating about the desires and effects of infidelity however may not only last but may also take a couple's relationship to quite possibly a whole new level.

Chapter Four
Let's Stop The Bullshit

When it comes to cheating, the general consensus is that it only or mostly occurs because women's emotional needs are not being met or because men are just men. Now I don't mean to contradict the many therapists and so – called relationship experts running amok but this to me is bullshit in its purest form. A person can spew all the men are from one planet, women are from another mess they want to but the bottom line is people's desires are basically the same. They want to be happy. What makes many people unhappy is that too many of them live according not to what they see and experience but according to what **others** have seen and heard. Their belief system is set in stone, so to speak and nothing short of an act of God will change it. People are allowed to believe whatever they want to. It's one of the perks of living in a free society and having free will. The bad thing about this is the fact that beliefs are only as true as the investigative qualities of an individual. For instance, if a woman believes all men ain't shit, then very few people in this world will be able to change her mind – especially a man. Now everybody in this world knows or should know that it is entirely unfair to generalize any group of individuals, whether that group be based on gender, race or otherwise. Unfortunately people still do it. It's one of those things that will never change, no matter how long this world is in existence. If a man believes women are unworthy of trust, again, there is little anyone will be able to say or do to prove otherwise. Beliefs are far too often based on an individual's hearsay as opposed to fact. As far as the emotional and physical aspects of relationships go, I believe the differences are few and far in between. Men have emotional issues they deal with all the time. Women get horny. There is no 'I can't do this' or 'I can't feel this way because I am of a particular gender. There is however the 'I can't let anybody know I feel this way because the historical beliefs of society would label me an outcast if I do.' Like I stated previously, what a crock!' This crock extends to 'if you're a man and you show any kind of emotion other than aggressive, then you're weak' and 'if you're a woman and you have what can be interpreted by most of this sometimes morally oppressive world as lusty desires, then you're a tramp.' These perceptions are what kills many relationships and are also what helps to cloud society's thinking when it comes to gender differences. The bottom line here is no one thing applies to everybody – especially in relationships. Women can cheat for a multitude of reasons, just like men - only problem the reasons are not always as politically correct as everybody believes they should be. On a personal note, I know several women who openly and often express their sexually desires, as in 'I need some dick!' Question: does that statement make them any less of a woman because of how they express themselves? Is it not the same as or almost the same as 'I'm in need of a particular type of relationship?' That relationship being a purely sexual one. People all too often expect things to be a certain way and when they're not, they are interpreted as wrong. If a man cries at a movie, does that make him less of a man? No. But ask ninety percent of his male friends and I am almost absolutely certain they will all agree it does. This world is so screwed up that if a person does not fit into society's accepted rules for behavior and existence, then that person is wrong. I am not saying that any man should start crying at the movies or that any woman should go around chanting 'I want dick and I want it now!' What I am saying is that if people were more honest and open with their feelings, desires and beliefs, there would not be half as many mistaken perceptions and fake relationships in this world.

Continuing with political correctness, one of the bigger reasons I have noticed women having for indulging in affairs is the size issue. If a woman is in love with a man who has a smaller penis than what she is used to, what reason is there for her to stay in that relationship? People profess love all the time but many of them are doing little more than just uttering the words. As much a part of happiness in relationships as sex is nowadays, unless the relationship itself is one where there is no sexual activity involved, few people will stand for sacrificing that level of happiness. Using the methods of historical belief, men are thought to have no control whatsoever when it comes to sexual intercourse. Men are thought to be mindless, orgasm driven, drones, whose dicks take over their brains when it comes to the pursuit of a woman. The big belief with men is that if they are not having enough sex, then their relationship is destined to fail. This is a ginormous problem because many in relationships feel that if a man is unhappy, all that is necessary to rectify any problem he may be having is a romp in the sack. It is not even thought of that there may be some underlying emotional factor, which may be causing the unhappiness. Then, when the man goes and has sex with somebody else, the belief is 'that's what men do anyway because they're dogs.' Maybe men need more understanding and less labeling. As long as people continue to believe that women do not desire sex as much as men do and for many of the same reasons men do, as well as believe that men have no emotion or are incapable of showing emotion, there will be continued misunderstanding and unhappiness in relationships. Here's a question I enjoy asking because almost nobody can come anywhere near to getting it right; how many men in this world who actively enjoy sexual intercourse, set out with the express intention of making a woman achieve an orgasm? 0. Okay I was being a little harsh. The actual number I believe is somewhere closer to about 3 or 4 - per state. Many men view sex as 'I am going to pound away at this woman until I achieve orgasm and if the woman I'm pounding away at should happen to achieve an orgasm during my pounding session, then I have achieved greatness. I should be placed in the Guinness book of world records somewhere near the man who can lift a car.' A lot of men actually believe that this is all a happy sexual encounter entails. Women have to shoulder some of the responsibility for men thinking as they do because when many teenagers start out having sex, they care not about making a woman feel good, they care about themselves feeling good. Often women participate in the 'act' because it feels good at the time but as people change so do their feelings as well as what makes them feel good. If a young man is taught that just banging a woman senseless is all which is necessary to make her happy, that belief will grow into adulthood. Then, when the woman begins complaining that sex is boring and mechanical; the man will think that something is wrong with her; that she has somehow changed. People in relationships don't really focus on issues so much until they become problematic in the relationship. It's the same thing with parents who never hit or discipline their children until the kids push one of those parents just an inch too far and the parent responds by beating the living shit out of the child and then not only is the parent labeled an abuser, that parent has to face the possibility of losing said child – all because of a temporary loss of control, which came about by the parent not taking the time to focus on and correct said issues when they were small. Then enter the options for relationship correction, such as nosey girlfriend therapy, counseling sessions, sex surrogates, etc. I don't mean to dog men as a whole but when they are young, often they feel as if it is a status symbol to sleep with a lot of women. The more they sleep with, the higher and faster they climb the social ladder, especially if these women are very attractive. Because sex between young people is often looked upon as taboo, many of them hide their activities from older, more experienced people who could help them make the experience more pleasurable for both parties, thereby creating the belief that as long as sex is being had, its being enjoyed. Sometimes men need to put themselves in the shoes of women to get a clearer understanding of why they respond to certain situations in the manner in which they do. When sex is new, it's easier to enjoy it more. One reason is because people are less restrictive and more willing to experiment in order to make their new partner enjoy the experience as much as possible. It's when the repetition sets in – that's what makes a person not enjoy it anymore and desire or at least contemplate infidelity. If a committed woman feels that all her man wants to do is have sex and in the same positions every day, what is logically going to happen when someone new comes along who wants not only to make love to her but wants to do it only how she wants or in a manner that she is not used to? A lot of women have this complaint that after so long, sex becomes as monotonous as someone playing a drum – the same thing, bam, bam, bam. That's not enjoyable because when you do the same thing time after time, year after year, <u>anybody</u> will tire of it. That is not what a relationship should entail. That is a job. Most of the people I know hate their jobs and why? Monotony. I love using contract security as an example because I have done it for so long and it is one of the worst professions I can think of. The question I have is how can a person stand or sit in one spot for seven to eight hours a day, day after day, month after month, year after year and not be bored out of his or her blinking mind? There has to be some severe mental conditioning needed to accomplish this or some severe mental damage. When I worked security, I had to do as outlined above, with no newspapers, no television, no Internet. One of the ways I survived was by imagining or fantasizing if you will of happier times, better jobs or what I was going to do once I got off duty. People in relationships often make sex a job as described above and then are left with basically the same options as I used to have. They fantasize of happier times, better partners or what they will do when the sex is over. This is where the moral factor comes in. Some men put their personal happiness over the feelings of their families. I understand how it happens because as a man I may have cheated one or two or three hundred times (just joking!) but women have this standard to uphold. They, I'm pretty sure, desire the change that we as men do but they can't do it as easily or as much as we can because of reputation. The difference here is that men rarely give a damn about reputation. That doesn't mean that men cheat more, it just means that we don't care if you think we do. Women get away with cheating for one simple reason and it's not because of the ever popular belief that they are better at what they do than men. It is because women are not expected to commit that type of indiscretion in the first place. Women are believed to be the weaker sex, the less intelligent counterpart or in short, the always innocent one. What should be remembered by people in general is that there is no innocence when it comes to infidelity – only massive deception. Both parties often cheat on one other but the rules of the game dictate that the one who portrays himself as the unfortunate and unknowing victim is the winner. A married woman could have sex every day with every man on her job and make the raunchiest x – rated videos of those encounters imaginable. Her husband, on the other hand, could have sex with one woman whom the husband, in a bout of overwhelming emotional guilt, tells the wife about. If the wife or her sex partners never divulge the specifics of their encounters, who will be deemed the whore? You guessed it, Mr. husband. And the funny thing about this is that the winner in this competition will almost never divulge the fact that he or she was even a player. He or she will play innocent until the day of death.

(All this deception in relationships and people wonder why so many of them end in divorce or separation. Go figure!)

One thing that people in relationships who get caught cheating often do is say 'It didn't mean anything.' This has to be the understatement of the millennium. Of course it didn't mean anything, what better excuse or justification can a person come up with? Using this excuse softens the blow somewhat because it lets the hurt party know that the guilty party's heart was not involved in the affair. And believe it or not people care more about knowing the heart was not involved because it allows for a better chance at possible reconciliation. If a person were to say that he or she loved the person he or she cheated with, the innocent party would more than likely believe or assume that the present relationship is over. Is this excuse believable? Most would say not but I tend to disagree with most depending upon the circumstances. What too many people do nowadays and have been doing for umpteen years is letting themselves go completely to pieces when they find out that their partners have been involved in an affair. Granted, being the unwitting victim in a relationship where there is infidelity hurts like hell but far too often people let this one infraction rule and ruin their lives. I know, as most people should, that there are countless reasons for a person committing infidelity. BUT a person, even if they do not know each and every possible cause, should know that there is a possibility and in some cases a high probability of it occurring. Some people feel that their relationships are above the possibility of infidelity. These people feel that sex is everlasting and always new and always whatever else which will leave no reason for the significant other to ever think about cheating. If and when a person just happens to cheat after however long, there is no understanding, no sympathy, just hatred and animosity because the thought is there that since you were faithful for so long, you should continue to be faithful for the rest of your natural life. These people either forget or do not realize in the first place that everything in life, even if done with super duper extreme type moderation, will become monotonous, if done long enough. I have to go back to chapter two of **The Correct Way To Fool Around** part one, for a minute –

Sex is like snow
You never know exactly how much you will get

Or exactly how long it will last.

This saying only applies to people who are not in committed relationships. People in committed relationships quickly or eventually become creatures of habit. They do the same positions, in the same areas of the house and unless one of the two complains, they will continue to do the same positions, in the same areas of the house <u>until</u> one of the two actually complains. The bad thing about this level of complacency is that people in relationships most often want to eliminate problems and many of those people want to eliminate these problems before they begin. They do this by not saying anything. The belief is if I don't say anything and my partner doesn't say anything, we will subconsciously trick each other into believing that nothing is wrong and we will continue to have the same boring ass, unfulfilling sex we have been having. One of the problems is that when one person in a relationship complains about a particular activity, which is being done by the other, to rectify the situation the other will often stop the activity all together, when in actuality, all that is needed is just a little adjustment. Ever notice how when a married man complains about his wife's proficiency when it comes to giving a blowjob, the wife slowly but surely eases away from that activity? To wit: 'you don't like the way I suck your dick? Okay I won't do it anymore! Go find some bitch on the street that does it better!' Then when the guy with the chapped penis does go and find a bitch on the street that coincidently does do it better and the wife finds out, she gets mad. What nerve! I do not want people for one second to believe that I am taking sides in this infidelity thing but if she only switched up the technique instead of totally flipping the script, maybe they'd still be together, maybe they'd still be having sex and maybe they'd still be happy. In a situation such as this when a person gets caught and says it didn't mean anything, what that person is really saying is 'honey I love you first and foremost. Second, nothing in or relationship has changed – that much. Third, I just had a little fun, kinda the same way a recovering alcoholic would sneak a bottle of rum into AA.' The thing that AA and infidelity have in common in this example is that both can change a person's life. AA can change a person's life if said person was to give up alcohol completely – and infidelity can change a person's life from the change that commitment can force it into being. Sneaking that bottle into an AA meeting does not always mean that person has irreparably damaged his or her chances at a clean and sober life just as having one adulterous liaison will not always irreparably damage the union. Sometimes a person in a committed relationship just wants to get his or her rocks off because the husband or wife is for whatever reason, preventing the spouse from obtaining that goal. A spouse, it should be stated, who seems to be preventing the partner from achieving the goal of getting his or her rocks off, is not always doing it intentionally. Many times people in relationships don't have sex because they have things on their minds – and not just things like 'I missed a bill, so now my perfect credit will be adversely affected.' These people have things on their minds like 'I lost my job and I may go homeless because I have no savings or family or plan b.' In addition to that; my significant other wants to have sex. And they wonder why that person is not in the mood or can't properly perform. Another thing, which goes with the statement above, is the fact that people are only going to find others attractive for a certain amount of time. A person will not be able to draw the same type of crowd at forty that they did twenty years before. A person should not be subject to anybody else's unfair or cruel and unusual punishment because he or she does not want to indulge in physical intimacy anymore. Note: I am not against marriage; I am just against people forcing change upon others. When people do this, forcing change, how can it possibly be expected that no one will cheat? This is the equivalent of giving a crying baby a pacifier, waiting until the exact moment the child stops crying, then taking it away and expecting that baby not to cry anymore. There are going to be repercussions to every action in this world, some favorable, some not. People have to understand that when you dangle a piece of meat in front of a hungry lion, said lion will make an attempt for said piece of meat. People cannot expect a person to be forever turned off from sex with other people once he or she gets committed, especially if he or she wasn't that way before the commitment. Sometimes 'it didn't mean anything' means it was just sex, no feeling, no commitment, just an orgasm or quite possibly, just the opportunity to bump uglies with somebody new. When a person has this level of understanding, more than likely, if the person he or she is involved with has an affair, there will not be such an extreme level of hurt. A person will more than likely be mad as hell, don't get me wrong but it will be nowhere near the point of not being able to recover. This is not the same as he's a man; he's going to cheat anyway or she's a woman and my last girl cheated on me; so she will too.' This is 'I understand that the possibility will always exist for infidelity. Whether I have sexual relations with my partner forty times a week or whether I have sex with him or her forty times a year, the possibility will always exist.' In this world, few things are new. The one thing, however which seems to constantly reinvent itself is the number of ways people lull themselves into complacency. Don't for one minute think that anyone in this world is above doing wrong, not even for one split second because once a person lets those defenses down, that will be the exact time those common sense shattering emotions will sneak in. Think about everybody in this world you know, I mean every single solitary person you have ever met. Now ask yourself, how many of those people have never made a mistake or done something wrong? You can't find any either, huh? The point I am trying to make when it comes to infidelity is you can choose to forgive or not but choosing to put a significant other on a pedestal high above the rest of the human race is ludicrous. Everybody is capable of failure, especially those who lie and tell you things like 'I will never cheat on you.' The sentiment sounds nice and all but you must be smarter than that. Love and or lust will always cloud common sense. At the end of The Correct Way To Fool Around, part one, chapter two, I mentioned that there is only one way to guarantee not getting caught in any kind of infidelity trap and that way is simply not to become involved in a relationship. One of the biggest problems with this is the fact that many people in this world have different criteria regarding what actually constitutes a relationship. There are those who believe a relationship starts the moment a man asks a woman for her hand and she says yes. There are others who believe in the 'assumed relationship' philosophy. This can get confusing because when in the 'assumed relationship' philosophy mindset, one person will assume that a relationship begins at the first sexual experience, whereas the other person will assume they are just fucking. This is where that little word with the ginormous meaning comes into play - communication. If this communication or miscommunication continues, the couple will eventually develop deep feelings for each other. One will continue with the feelings of 'our relationship is growing deeper everyday' and the other will continue with feelings of 'why does this person keep trying to pressure me into a relationship? I thought he or she understood that we were just fucking.' Love a person with your head, not your heart. Find out if you are in fact in a relationship so that there will be no misunderstanding about actual cheating and the resemblance of. Use the logic of a smart car buyer; 'I just bought a brand new car, I don't expect it to last forever but I plan to enjoy it every day until it either dies, involves itself in an accident or leaves. (Due to theft.) This type of mindset will not prepare a person for everything life has to offer but it will soften the blow for certain things. Believing that something in this world lasts forever is pure and unequivocal bullshit – especially the commitment factor in relationships. Remember the title of this chapter people – 'Let's Stop The Bullshit!'

Chapter Five
Conquering And Being Conquered

For the longest of time, anything relating to pornography, whether it be strip clubs, x – rated videos or what have you, has been deemed offensive or degrading to women. Even certain positions within the act of sexual intercourse itself have come under fire as being an act only or mostly enjoyed by the man. If a man and woman are embracing, with him on top and her underneath during intercourse, then it's looked upon by most as lovemaking. If a man is behind the woman and pounding away, then it's looked at as fucking and not only is it fucking but it is viewed as the man dominating the woman. Many people no longer see sex as a mutual activity. It is more a 'I'm doing this to you for my own personal gratification, while you're letting me do this to you for your own agenda.' I want people to think about something for a second; why is it that almost every father in the world will get mad when a man takes advantage of his little girl but almost every father of a boy praises that boy when he takes advantage of someone else's?' Is it because a woman has a reputation to uphold or such is the belief? A man is, has and always will be seen as the one dominating the act of sex. Whether the man is good in bed or not is not even thought of as an issue. As long as he and a woman are intimate, the belief will be he did something to the woman and the woman had something done to her. This is the theory behind conquering and being conquered. Women have always been thought of as being submissive. Most men know this is not always true, especially of married women but the belief is there. Men, because they are endowed with the particular anatomical structure, with which they are, are believed to be aggressive dogs that only conquer as many submissive women as possible. Women do not take advantage of men. Correction - let me rephrase that. Women do take advantage of men but they do it in different ways than men do to them. If sex or 'lovemaking' were actually thought of as an equal partnership activity, many pregnant women would never be saying things like 'you did this to me!' they would be saying things like 'look at how beautiful the life we created together is growing.' Men would not be saying things like 'I broke her back!' or 'I think you're just taking advantage of my daughter' They would be saying things like 'I can't wait to get married so that we can consummate our union.' Forgive me for not being politically correct here but no one ever hears a woman saying 'I fucked the shit out of that man!' This is why the double standard exists. Men, for reasons unknown, do not have to define their actions. The only explanation, which is necessary, is the mere fact that a man is a man. Many people or should I say, many disillusioned people in this world, would like to believe that sex or 'lovemaking' is a sharing of emotions or as stated before, an 'equal partnership activity.' The bottom line here is that men are the ones doing the fucking and the women are the ones getting fucked - sometimes in more ways than one. Earlier in this passage I mentioned that fathers get upset when they believe their daughters are being taken advantage of. This is understandable as any parent who has concern for his or her child would. But sometimes the advantage taking is nothing more than a historical and societal based belief. Taking advantage is usually defined as a person benefiting from the lack of education or lack of resources of others. If a person allows something to be done to them while fully aware of the ramifications, that is not being taken advantage of. It is most often letting people think that that person is being taken advantage of. Sometimes the sex between daddy's little girl and the captain of the football team is consensual and sometimes, surprisingly, is initiated by the female. One of the truly messed up things about this world is that people too often do what society has done or what society will have them do to gain or maintain acceptance. When it comes to taking advantage, while men are seen as conquerors in the sexual arena, women are seen as masters in the mental one. The mind games, the infidelity and the procurement of gifts, rent payments or general upkeep is believed to be because one; the men know no better and two; the men wish to be able to continue to conquer the women in the bedroom. <u>Life is a game.</u> Men have their strengths, women do to but neither gender ever really wins. Neither gender ever really conquers. What drives many people in this world is reputation. It can make or break a relationship, as well as a person's life. If at the age of thirteen, a young man makes a mistake and steals from a church and the event happens to be captured on camera and publicized, chances are that years down the line, people who know or know of this man will believe that he is forever nothing more than a thief. Many of those people will believe that this individual is incapable of change. His chances at politics, if he should so choose that profession, will be ironically lowered. Most of the jobs this man applies for will require a background check and depending upon how publicized his teenage incident was, he may never be able to get a 'good' job or at least not one dealing with money. The reason for this blacklisting is due to reputation. As stated before, a reputation will make or break a relationship, as well as an individual's life. If a married woman were to regularly beat up her husband, they would both garner a reputation, an unpleasant one for the woman but definitely an unfavorable one for the man. When it comes to infidelity, no one desires to be the innocent victim because that would mean that said person was the one who got 'played.' Nobody wants to get played, no matter the circumstances because then he or she develops a reputation of gullibility or stupidity. People will rather kill somebody than have the reputation of being gullible and or stupid because once a person has this type of reputation, others will form in their minds opinions of who conquered whom. And whether these opinions are right or wrong, just the fact that they are given as labels, makes them much more damaging.

A relationship is, as often thought, supposed to be fifty-fifty. This means whatever one person does in that relationship, so should the other – or at least be able to. When the odds shift to either side, there exists a level of control. This level of control can be seen as one person being able to conquer the other. If a person continuously or even one time, cheats on another and gets away with it or is allowed to get away with it, then that person is seen as having ultimate control, the one who has conquered.

Chapter Six
Infidelity; The Victim & The Perpetrator

If a person were to take a worldwide survey on who is happier when it comes to infidelity, meaning the victim or the perpetrator, a safe bet would probably be the perpetrator. At first glance, many people would be inclined to agree, especially when you consider the potential perks. One of those perks includes having sex with someone new or somebody different. Another perk is the momentary and sometimes long lasting escape that infidelity provides. And yet still another perk is the level of excitement, which comes along with knowing that a person has gotten away with murder – so to speak. Let's forget for a moment that men are almost always viewed as the aggressors and or initiators when it comes to infidelity and examine the effects of and on both.

The Victim

The word victim encompasses many things. It is the definition given to somebody who is hurt or killed by somebody or something. It is also somebody that is harmed by an act or circumstance. Still another definition states that a victim is somebody who experiences misfortune and feels helpless to do anything about it. When infidelity occurs, unless it's some new type of robotic Internet porn, it's usually between two people – the gender doesn't matter these days – the bottom line is one person who is in a relationship is having sexual relations with someone who may or may not be in a relationship of his or her own. The individual who is not having sex outside the relationship or who does not get caught having sex outside the relationship is also granted the title of victim. A victim can be innocent or willing. An innocent victim is the easiest to identify. He or she is the one who knows little or nothing of the infidelity, which is taking place. The innocent victim is kept in the dark so to speak because of several reasons. One reason could be that he or she is too honest and pure of heart to believe that the level of deception which infidelity requires is actually present in his or her relationship. Another reason could be that the innocent victim is not capable of understanding the fact that infidelity is actually occurring. Let me elaborate – the innocent victim is usually completely capable of understanding that infidelity may be occurring but he or she is not always completely capable of understanding that he or she has a choice in whether or not to accept the infidelity, which is or may be occurring. This is one reason why many people deal with those who are or who seem less intelligent than themselves. These people feel that they can just manipulate the mind of the person they are involved with like the mind was made out of silly puddy. Still another reason people are kept in the dark is because they care not to know. These people are intelligent. They are also open minded enough to know that infidelity is always a possibility but they close their minds when the topic of infidelity actually affecting their own relationship comes up. They choose to be kept in the dark rather than face the pain of knowing their significant other is being unfaithful.

The willing victim knows infidelity is going on but he or she feels helpless to do anything about it. He or she feels helpless because not only has he accepted the infidelity; he allows it to continue. In many relationships people put up with things, which are not in their best interests and many times people put up with things which are detrimental to the relationship as well as to the person's existence. 'Willing victims' in relationships will put up with things like a partner smoking when they themselves don't or will deal with that partner having an illegal gun in the house when they themselves abhor violence or anything connected with it because in the grand scheme of the relationship, those infractions are relatively small. Most people know or should know that smoking increases the chance for complications, which will lead to a person's death – just as the same amount of people should know that having a gun in the home increases the chance of an accidental shooting or death. Yet these things are tolerated because usually every other or mostly every other aspect of the person or the relationship is going well. The people who put up with these gun possessing smokers may in fact be the total opposite of them but they feel that it would cost them more in the long run if they were to lose them now. Infidelity hurts the willing victim because it forces the victim to constantly make excuses for the perpetrator's actions. It will cause the willing victim to say things like 'I know he's cheating but he takes care of my kids as well as my unemployed behind so it's really not so bad.' Victims of infidelity suffer in many ways. One of the biggest ways in which they suffer besides putting up with a person who is in fact cheating is by not knowing whether or not the cheating is just an outlet for frustration or whether it is possibly a precursor to that party falling in love with the person he or she is cheating with. I mean let's face it; most of the relationships today are not started like those back in the '50's where a man courts a woman for x amount of days, weeks or months, followed by the man meeting the girl's parents and family, then followed by the proposal and then eventually the marriage and then the sex. No, most relationships are started by a couple finding that initial attraction, discussing what they like and what they have in common, letting their girlfriends and best friends know that they've found a hot guy or girl, then comes the sex. So yeah, the victim definitely has a legitimate concern when it comes to infidelity. With the new updated schedule of relationships, a couple can fall in love within a week and the innocent victim can be sitting at home thinking 'I know he's playing the field but as long as I'm number one' or 'as long as he comes home, I'm okay with it.' The problem with this is that nobody really knows what reaction will be caused by any action. The person playing the field could actually fall in 'love' and fall in 'love' head over heels – and not only that but leave his family and family life behind in an instant. I put the word love in quotes because as we all know love is not something which happens overnight. It is not something that occurs when a man whispers sweet nothings into a woman's ear nor is it something that happens when good sex is had. Love takes time. Lust is what happens overnight. Lust makes a person believe there is love close by. When a person meets someone new and instantly leaves or desires to leave his or her family because of that new person, it is not because that new person has captured their heart with an unbreakable hold of affection. It is likely because there were or are issues in the relationship which need fixing. Some victims have been quoted as saying 'I know he's cheating but I'm gonna wait and give him just enough rope to hang himself so that I can have the pleasure of watching him feel guilty and come running back to me with his tail between his legs so to speak. This is wrong. This is wrong on so many levels because a person <u>never</u> knows how far another's heart may or may not actually be gone. Really hate to beat a dead horse here but ongoing communication in relationships is ESSENTIAL! Without it you are just fucking. Sorry for being blunt but that's what it is. You are opening up a Pandora's box of potential problems because everybody in a relationship will at one time or another find something about the significant other that they do not particularly care for. When you do not make the person you are involved with aware of what may be troubling to you, that person more than likely may continue to do what is troublesome to you. This is not rocket science. This is not new. What this is can be described as one of the most basic problems of infidelity. Even though as I have stated many times before in my prior works, a relationship is never between just two people; the communication must be. It cannot – no it must not be a thing of boy meets girl, boy loves girl, boy cannot talk to girl for whatever reason, so girl discusses all of her problems with her girlfriends. A relationship never includes just two people. It most often includes many of the people that each party in the relationship knows. The people in the relationship must be smart enough to keep these people out of the relationship because if not, the two cents, which everybody in this world loves to give, will determine how the relationship goes – especially when it comes to infidelity. Historically when infidelity has occurred, friends of the victim will side with the victim and not because the victim is right or wrong but because of the simple fact that the victim is the victim. This is bad because many times when infidelity occurs, the victim desires comforting more than anything. Of course the victim will want to know why it happened and what if anything he or she did to contributing to its happening but the first thing someone who has been scarred by an affair wants is healing. All friends are going to do is place blame on the ones who committed the transgression, while attempting to make the victim seem like he or she was so innocent. Don't get me wrong – a transgression can be 99% the fault of the person who initiated the affair but some blame must be attributed to the other party. Just as with a happy relationship, both parties are responsible – the same thing holds true for one where there is infidelity.

The Perpetrator

The word perpetrator is simple. It is mainly defined as one who commits or is responsible for something, usually something criminally or morally wrong. To put it simply; the one who did it. In the case of infidelity, the perpetrator is the one who usually has all the fun. To perpetrate the crime of infidelity, one must usually follow certain steps. The first is usually to target his objective. This means a person has to find someone with whom the proposed infidelity is to occur. This can happen by a number of ways; either the perpetrator initially plans out his attack, even down to the type of individual he wants to have the affair with or he may just happen to luck up with some loose moral having individual who shares his diabolical plan of deceit. After finding the objective, the perpetrator then has the task of planning exactly how he will get his objective in bed. This can happen by the perpetrator actually devising a step by step procedure to get the intended target to succumb to his will or it could be accomplished by the perpetrator using some silver tongued devil type of rhetoric, more commonly known as running game. If the perpetrator is successful in getting the intended target to fall for his malarkey, he will then have to devise a secondary plan to prevent himself from getting caught by his part time private eye significant other. This may seem like an excessive amount of work - the searching, the planning, and the secondary planning but to the experienced philanderer, it is nothing but a walk in the park. The perpetrator is the one with the power. He is the one who controls the situation of infidelity, as he is also the one who states how long the proposed infidelity is to last and how said infidelity is to be carried out. Understand that the usage of the word he does not by any means imply that all infidelity is initiated or carried out by men. Most people in relationships know all too well that this is not true. Perpetrators come in all shapes, sizes, colors and genders. It must be mentioned however that the female perpetrator is different from the male. Whereas male perpetrators often come off as aggressive, player types, the females are many times subtle in their pursuits. The female perpetrator will lure the male seductively and deceptively to make it seem as if the infidelity is actually being perpetrated by the male. Male perpetrators may attempt to beat around the bush when it comes to pursuing their objectives but do to the fact that they are men, many of their objectives expect to be hit with some type of game anyway. This is one of the few down sides that male perpetrators face. Men are historically the ones who initiate infidelity as well as the ones who get busted in the act of infidelity more often than women – so when a prospective objective sees them coming, if they are smart, they will be able to spot the game so to speak a mile away. This is also why many of the male perpetrators play the shy role. Some women love to take control in relationships – especially when they find what appears to be an easy mark. Many 'players' will approach a woman with the same old tired story of 'my significant other and I love each other but there's no sex being had in the relationship. We're just together for the sake of the kids.' Women can see through that shit like it's water. What women don't expect is for a man not to pursue them. When they encounter this, they most often assume that a) the man is religious. b) the man is gay or c) the man is shy. The female perpetrator is many times more successful than her counterpart because historically woman have been viewed as the weaker sex, the less intelligent sex or the ones whose instincts were so maternal that they were almost incapable of doing wrong. You see historically and even to this day, when it comes to the initiating or enjoyment of the sex act, men are supposed to be the only ones doing it. When a woman has sex out of wedlock or has an extramarital affair, she is never looked at as a person who just wants to have a little fun – she is looked at like Hester Prynne. Female perpetrators have this ready made disguise, which they can don at any time – especially if they are accused of being the initiator of an affair. They can say something as simple as 'I was just being nice and he took it the wrong way.'

Most of the time the perpetrator is at fault when infidelity occurs but there are exceptions. Sometimes the victim and the perpetrator can both be at fault. The longstanding belief is that whenever a person in a relationship cheats, that person is completely wrong and solely the blame. What is almost never examined is the possibility that maybe and quite possibly the so called innocent party could have contributed to the infidelity a lot more than he or she would like to believe. A person can contribute to infidelity in many ways. One of the most popular ways a person can contribute to the destruction of his or her relationship is by the constructive abandonment thing. From my understanding, this entails one part of a seemingly happy couple not indulging in the act of sexual intercourse with the other. Except for medical reasons, religion and monotony, this is one thing I could never understand. People get married and almost 100% of the time sex between the parties is enjoyed. Then, sometime down the line sex becomes a reward – a bargaining chip if you will. Does this mean that one person does not like sexual intercourse anymore or does it mean that that person does not like sex anymore with his or her significant other? When does sex change from 'let's make love' to 'I'll give you some?' This resembles 'I'm doing you a favor by having sex with you and if I don't feel like doing it for whatever reason or for whatever length of time, you have no choice but to wait until I do.' In a situation as described above both parties can be seen as the ones who were at fault. The innocent victim is at fault because he or she basically prevented the perpetrator from enjoying relations with him or her as well as drove the perpetrator to commit the indiscretion by holding out. The perpetrator is at fault because even though they were extenuating circumstances, which led to the infidelity occurring, the perpetrator had an obligation to remain faithful no matter what. (Till death do part and all that crap) This is why I believe annulments should be available all throughout a person's marriage. The only stipulation is unlike divorce you only get from the relationship what you came into it with. This could be a very acceptable alternative to divorce. (or maybe I'm just rambling again!)

It should be understood that the perpetrator of infidelity, although many times unnoticeable, has problems. He is hurting because he or she is unhappy. The infidelity is one of the only outlets the perpetrator has, which temporarily relieves the problems the cheater is presently having. People loved to be classified as a player or the one who can cheat and never get caught but a person has to sit down and examine not the fact that a person does something but why. I know many people today who are involved in adulterous unions. When I speak of adulterous unions, I am talking about on both ends of the spectrum – from being married while having a steady sex partner on the side to being committed while sleeping with everybody they can get their penis - I mean hands on. In many of these relationships, there has been no solid grounding on with which to build – no religious foundation, no relationship instruction from parents, just two people who feel that as long as the sex is good and the necessary money is there, there should be no problems in the relationship. There were several occasions where I had the opportunity to spend several days with some of the couples where at least one partner was cheating and I don't know if it was a personal thing against me but there was almost no talking in the household. If there was any conversation at all, it was general as in 'what's for dinner' or 'anybody call?' Granted most of these couples were married or together for a significant amount of years but in my opinion that should give people more to talk about not less. Didn't seem that way. In other relationships I found that the same thing was occurring. The conversations were different but they were little more than 'how was your day?' followed by a few questions and some quality time with the kids, then it was off to their respective roles – the female on the phone with her girlfriends and the male in front of the television. I would ask the couples, separately of course, 'don't you two ever go out together' and the responses were almost always the same; 'he doesn't want to go anywhere with me' or she'd rather go hang out with her girlfriends.' I would then ask each of them did you try asking and again the responses would be almost always the same; 'I don't like to do the things he likes to do' or 'she only wants to go where her girlfriends are going to be.' This made me wonder what happened when these couples first got together? I mean obviously there had to have been some kind of interaction besides sexual, right? There must have been some sort of going out or getting to know period. If two people, during this period did not like the things each other was doing or interested in, why would the relationship be allowed to continue? Was it that the relationship was all a farce? Was it nothing more than 'I'll do what this person likes so that I can get them into bed or so that I can get what I want out of this relationship? Or is it that they just grow apart? I have a very unpopular philosophy regarding unhappiness in relationships – it goes 'if you're unhappy, leave.' Very simple – straight and to the point. The problem with people using my strategy is that they have let life get in the way of their relationships. They have let kids, family, finances and whatever else ruin the happiness and spontaneity they once had. They have become, dare I say it, complacent. And as if complacency weren't bad enough, these people feel that since they can't do anything about it together, they take on the responsibility of making themselves happy. Unfortunately cheating is one of the most often thought of ways for a person to be happy. It's not that every time there is a seemingly insurmountable problem in a relationship, a person sets out to cheat – it's that there are too few other options that a person is willing to employ. People need outlets. These outlets can be talking to girlfriends on the phone, going to strip clubs or maybe just hanging out with the opposite sex to get a different perspective on one's relationship. The problem with these outlets is that the more a person involves himself or herself, the more chance there is to become addicted. Addiction is never good. Addiction to strip clubs causes people to lose money, which could and quite possible should be used for family. Addiction to discussing problems on the phone can lead to people putting more of their two cents in than what's necessary. This can lead to a person being influenced and actually trying to live their relationship the way a friend has suggested. Many times talking on the phone can lead to 'hey why don't you come to this get together I'm having with some real cute members of the opposite sex.' Granted a person may have no intention at all on cheating but think about what will happen when said person accepts that invitation and goes to the get together and meets a member of the opposite sex who just happens to be so attentive and responsive to the needs of the person with the relationship problem? Simple, there will be an attraction. An attraction is how infidelity often starts.

Chapter Seven
An Open Mind Must Be Maintained When Confronting Or Combating Infidelity

Many people in this world believe that infidelity is the one thing from which there is no vindication. These people believe that once a person has partaken in the act of infidelity, that person has lost any and all resemblance to someone who is deserving of forgiveness. One of the truly wonderful things about this world is the fact that everyone has, along with free will, the ability to make up his or her mind in any manner he or she wishes. One of the truly sad things about this world is the fact that not everyone needs the same amount of motivation for his or her mind to go off into whatever direction he or she wants it to. This means that while one person needs absolute, clear and concise evidence to believe infidelity exists; the next person may need little more than to hear a rumor. When a person in a relationship is presented with the possibility of infidelity, his or her state of mind, as well as his or her present relationship will determine how quickly or not they believe the infidelity assumption is an actual fact. The fact that many people think that infidelity is the point of no return is what makes them judge, jury and executioner. Their belief is once it happens, the person who is accused of committing it is wrong and should be spayed or neutered. No questions. This closed minded mentality leaves no room for reconciliation or for proving innocence for that matter. An open mind is what is absolutely needed when unproven accusations arise. It must be a situation of innocent until proven guilty and not the other way around, as with many of the police officers in New York, for example. Situations, which resemble infidelity, can and often do surpass those of infidelity itself. These situations are many times the cause of breakups and if not breakups, then long lasting distrust and turmoil in the relationship. An open mind, when relating to infidelity, unlike its nemeses the closed mind, will allow a person to see possible and realistic scenarios as truth, as opposed to well thought out excuses. An open mind will allow an individual in a relationship to say maybe that person I don't know is an actual friend and not somebody my significant other is fucking. An open mind will also allow someone to say maybe traffic really is messed up every third Tuesday and that's why my wife is late – as opposed to 'the grimy bitch is screwing her boss once a month!' Now granted, having an open mind is not the same thing as seeing infidelity clear as day and attempting to dispel the fact that it exists. Having an open mind means 'I am aware that the possibility of infidelity exists but I am mature and wise enough to know that the possibility of infidelity existing does not mean that it is actually going on.

What many people don't always realize is that they unwittingly dictate the direction in which their relationships travel by the attitudes they possess. If a person has the attitude or belief of 'if you cheat on me, then you are 100% wrong and there's no way in heaven or hell that I will ever forgive you, then its pretty safe to say that if there ever was a case of infidelity, where one party had gotten caught, then the relationship is pretty much over. If a person has the attitude of "if I think you are cheating, then you are," again it's a pretty safe bet that that relationship is or will be over pretty soon as well. In today's society, with the constant bombardment of sexually explicit conversation, on television and in everyday life, as well as infidelity ruining other people's relationships at breakneck speeds, it's not that difficult for a person to believe that his or her significant other would fall victim to infidelity or at least temptation – especially with the help of those nosey, good for nothing friends that many of us presently have. As I have stated many times in my prior works, infidelity is a crime of sorts, rather a crime of passion. And just as with regular crime, there is always a perpetrator, a victim and usually an accomplice. If a crime is committed and no one knows the specifics (who, what, where etc.) and no one is hurt outright, it may very well be forgotten. If on the other hand a crime is committed and it is public knowledge and someone is hurt, there will likely be severe consequences. In either scenario, passing premature judgment is never the best way to go. If there's one certainty about life, it's this: the truth, no matter how depressing, no matter how damaging, no matter how unwelcome, will eventually come out. Spending time worrying about if infidelity has happened or if it will happen is pointless because if it's going to happen, it's going to happen.

Chapter Eight
The Perfect Crime

Is there really such a thing? This topic has been heavily debated by everyone, from college professors to law enforcement personnel the world over. Yet it's difficult for anyone to give a definitive answer. There have been at least a myriad of unsolved crimes in this world but are they perfect? Infidelity has long been deemed a victimless crime. It has even been called a harmless crime but can anyone indulging in it truly say they have attained perfection? Perfection is self-explanatory. It basically means the quality of something that is as good or suitable as it can possibly be, in other words, a quality that no human being can ever possess. To take a piece of the perfection definition in regards to infidelity, a person who commits infidelity, has to be as good as one possibly can in order to not get caught. Several years ago, there was committed one of the most expensive heists in recorded history. The heist netted over eight million dollars. For a while this was classified as the perfect crime. It was deemed so because the crooks were meticulous in their planning. The perpetrators broke into an unnamed bank through an adjacent building and over the course of a weekend, emptied out over eight million bucks. There was no trace of evidence, no fingerprints, no paper trail. It was almost the perfect crime. The crooks who perpetrated this crime hid out in a motel, which was also immaculately cleaned, except for one thing. The crooks ate! Not only did they eat, they put the dishes inside the dishwasher afterwards. Had they done one simple thing, they would probably still be free today. That one thing was turning the dishwasher on. DNA was able to be retrieved from the utensils the crooks used to eat and this is what led to their capture. Unbelievable isn't it? All the planning which more than likely went into perpetrating this crime went down the drain because no one remembered or thought enough to turn on the dishwasher. Does this mean that there is no perfect crime or does this mean that no one has yet taken the time to plan every detail of a crime to assure there is only the smallest iota of a chance of getting caught? The chances are pretty strong that those crooks will never see a free day again but just imagine if they had succeeded. If they had dispersed the money in such a way so as not to attract attention, meaning not immediately quitting their jobs, not purchasing all new items and not letting everyone know what they had done, they, their kids, and several generations would be happy beyond belief. Unfortunately nobody with the exception of several law enforcement entities and one particular bank is singing any praises. This can be best described as two opposite ends of a spectrum. On the one end, happiness beyond compare, on the other end, the worst earthly punishment imaginable. When you cheat, it may not be on such a grand scale as this but the consequences may share a spectrum of life and death. In other words, commit an indiscretion, whether planned or not, get away with it, and live to see another day and quite possibly commit another indiscretion. On the opposite end of the spectrum, commit an indiscretion, get caught and have your crazy in love significant other cut your dick off. What's possibly even worse is the off chance that your significant other may go ahead and kill the other woman, leaving you to wallow in guilt for the rest of your days. Either way it's a no win situation. To commit the perfect crime, an all or nothing mindset must be adopted, because more often than not, that's usually what it will be. Regarding infidelity, many will argue that its impossible to do it perfectly and they are well within their rights to believe that. But it's also possible that these doubting individuals don't or have never taken the time to do it right. To cheat correctly, one has to ask every question that they think their significant other will ask – and even ones their significant other will have no reason to ask. And then come up with a believable answer. The proverbial one step ahead philosophy does not apply here. Here, a person who commits infidelity must be two and even three steps in front of the significant other. When a person who is committing infidelity lies for instance, the lie should be based on or around an actual event, such as a birthday or prominent day in that person's life - that way a person will retain much more accurate information as opposed to just making up a complete lie from scratch. The difference with this is if you make up a lie out of the blue, just adding facts and figures as you go along, chances are very likely that in ten years or so down the line when your significant other gets bored and decides to bring it up again, you'll mess up and mess up big! If however you keep the event limited to your birthday for instance, chances are you will never forget the day the supposed indiscretion took place. Rule of thumb – keep lies simple! The more detailed the lie, the more chance you will have to forget specific details as the time progresses. Look at the difference between these two statements; 1) I went to the zoo on my birthday. 2) I went to the zoo on my birthday and while at the zoo, I saw the monkeys, penguins, lions and then I applied for a job at the zoo's concession stand, then saw a zoo security guard beat up a vagrant who was busted trying to steal a baby penguin and then…

Now both of these statements may in fact be true but the problem is as history has many times shown, the longer a period of time elapses, the easier it becomes to forget relevant or irrelevant facts. If questioned and a person uses the forgetful excuse, whether it is true or not, that person will more than likely be thought of as lying.

Another step in the perfect crime process is what should be done even before the act of infidelity is done and that is acting out the crime. Many will say this step is unnecessary but if more people in this world knew what they were going to do before a situation happens which leaves them wondering if he or she did it right or took the appropriate course of action, fewer people would go to jail, put their foot in their mouths or get caught cheating. To act out an affair, the first thing one needs to do is note the time. This is important because a person will have to be aware of how long they have to get the house back to normal before the significant other gets home. If the adulterer lives with the significant other, he or she will need to set a time frame for sex – meaning the physical activity cannot extend past thirty minutes, one hour, two hours or however long it may take. This is important because most people usually let the physical intimacy dictate how long the session is to last. In other words the parties involved usually do it until one or both reach their climactic point. Now if there was a time frame for the physical intimacy – meaning whether the couple reached their peaks or not – once the buzzer, alarm clock or mental time piece went off, the couple would know to get up, get dressed and get out, there would be few to no instances of 'my significant other walked in on us while we were screwing.' The next step is estimating the recovery time. By recovery time I speak of the time certain people need to recapture the wits and energy needed to get their orgasm weary asses up and out of your house. This can be anywhere from a few seconds to a few minutes or more. This is important because some people feel that after they have indulged you in a great love making session, they are owed time to cuddle, spoon or whatever – and this is bad because when a couple gets together in that romantic, after sex, hugging position, it is very easy to fall asleep. Trust me when I tell you there is no excuse a significant other will believe or is willing to hear when she comes home and finds the two of you naked. The next step is the clean up. This entails doing if need be, a room-to-room condom search and a wet spot search. We all know what wet spots are but what we all do not realize we sometimes do when we cheat is cover the wet spot with a either a new sheet or the same sheet. If you are smart enough (and I hope you are) to change the sheet, be mindful that quite often the wet spot has already saturated or will saturate the mattress, which in turn will saturate the new sheet that you put on. This will cause the significant other to ask why is the bed wet. Good luck explaining that! You can say you spilled something on the bed but what many who try to cover their tracks after committing an affair will do is throw on a new sheet and a new cover. If the cover is dry and the sheet below is wet due to moisture from the mattress, no doubt about it – you're busted. To circumvent this potential problem, use a mattress pad before you do the do. This way you can soak up any unwanted wet spots without having to worry about your significant other laying in one of them. Just don't keep the mattress pad in the house! I had unfortunately fallen victim to this brand of trickery. I was living with a trifling ex girlfriend a few years back and we had the type of employment schedules where we rarely saw each other. She worked in the morning and I worked at night. So basically, when I came in from work, she was heading out. Whatever intimacies we shared had to be nudged between the hour or so that stretched from the end of my shift to right before the beginning of hers. One day as luck would have it, I was relieved early and decided to go home and have an extended quickie. I arrived two hours early and found her in the shower. Normally I wouldn't think of a woman who is otherwise clean taking a shower as strange but I usually arrive home around seven. She was in the shower at five. Hmmm. Her answer to my inquisition about why she was up so early was 'I couldn't sleep.' Okay I figured I had no choice but to accept that because I had found nobody in the house nor did I have any prior reason to distrust her. I didn't focus too much on the fact that she said she didn't want to have sex because I figured if she couldn't sleep, it must have been due to some kind of minor medical issue (headache, insomnia, bad dream or something along those lines) and the not wanting to have sex must've just went right along with the ailments. Okay so I continued on to the bedroom. I kinda figured that if I just got naked and hopped in the bed, she would be a little more receptive and maybe give in to my pussy pursuit. But wait just a minute here! If she's in the shower already, why is the bed wet? I mean I could understand if she had just gotten out and decided to air dry by lying on the bed but that's not what happened at all. In fact I asked her that very question. 'Honey, did you leave the shower since you went into the bathroom?' she answered no. I didn't see any glasses in the sink or in the bedroom, which would have probably been consistent with her making up a story about spilling something. So after doing my own little bit of detective work, I just came out and asked her 'Honey, why is the bed wet?' She followed the protocol of a cheater to a 'T' – surprised look, pause before answering and the biggie…the stuttering. She said that she had spilled some juice on the bed but the juice we had was colored (not black for all you funny people) but red, blue etc. I figured that it wasn't completely outside of the realm of possibility for her to be telling the truth but if she were, why was it that I found no wet paper in the trash or no wet towel other than the one that she was using? She didn't bother to answer too many more of my questions – in fact she kinda got upset that I continued pressing her for information. Was I wrong? Who knows? Like I always tell people, the only sure way to tell if a person is or has been cheating is to catch that person in the act and since I didn't, I was left to forever wonder. But my conscience did bother me for many days after that incident. I guess it was one of those situations where we know better but we allow our minds to trick ourselves into believing that we're wrong or maybe it's just a situation, which resembles infidelity. I really believe she had someone in the bed that night but since I could not prove it I had to let it go. It bothered me but not half as much as the wonder of not knowing who actually caused that wet spot I was laying in; her or whoever she had in the bed. Disgusting thought! Another way you can get around this is to turn the mattress over. I know some of you may have these new fangled, expensive type of beds which don't allow for over-turning and for these types of beds all one would have to do is take a glass of liquid (preferably colored) into the bedroom and spill its contents over the wet area on the mattress. Make sure to leave some liquid in the glass and leave the glass in the bedroom. This way if you are questioned – and believe me you will be questioned, you can always say that you were in the process of cleaning up. If you happen to deal with one of those obsessive compulsive order having clean freaks like I normally do, who do not allow drinks in the bedroom you can always say that there was a news program on TV which you just had to see or the phone was ringing and while rushing to answer it, you made your unavoidable mess. Also, if you are smart enough to wash the sheets, make sure you wash other clothes too. (Not in the same load) A dead giveaway will be the fact that only the sheets were washed. If you wash your clothes, your significant other's clothes and the sheets, your significant other may actually believe that you were trying to make an honest effort at cleaning up the house instead of trying to just clean up after an indiscretion. Okay, we've covered noting the time, estimating recovery time and the clean up. The next and final step is getting your story straight. This may seem like an insignificant measure but it can have dire consequences if done in an incorrect manner. Here's a for instance:

'What did you do today honey?'
'Nothing, just watched television.'
'Did you take a nap?'
'No.'
'Then why are there new sheets on the bed?'

What possible answer can a person give that will not raise the suspicion level? When a person who did not prepare is in this situation, every possible delay tactic will be utilized. From the momentary pause to the 'what, you don't trust me or something?' Delay tactics are good but the problem that comes with using them in a surprise situation is that they often come as a surprise instead of a viable defense. When delay tactics are used in a surprise situation, the word duh comes into play – and stuttering almost always accompanies. This can be avoided by simply practicing. Practice the above steps in addition to whatever conversation you think will throw your significant other off. The conversation in no way has to be interesting or even true, just believable - otherwise the significant other will have reason to suspect. Here's how the situation above should have or could have gone:

'Hey honey, what did you do today?'

'I cleaned up a little bit, washed the clothes.'

'Why?'

I' just figured I would help' or 'I just wanted to surprise you' or 'you always say I never do anything.'

The excuses of just wanting to help or just wanting to surprise you are best reserved for someone who does not usually assist in cleaning up the home. This lie can best be assisted by continuing to clean up the home even after the significant other has arrived. Note; this behavior, especially if not expected, will cause a possible interrogation – not to mention the expectation of this type of behavior continuing. Committing the perfect crime, whether relating to infidelity or regular crime is never easy. It takes skill. It takes diligence – but it does not take superior intellect, as many like to believe. People would classify someone in the position of

Bill Gates or Oprah as having achieved perfection in their chosen fields but what these people do not realize is that they were not just handed the position they have in life. They, just as most of the rich people in this world I believe have had to work at what they do until they perfected it. The same thing applies to infidelity. You cannot just do it one time and say yep, now I'm an expert. If the act of infidelity is something you want to pursue, just remember that it, like every other venture in life has obstacles, traps and pitfalls. But if you want to succeed, you must be diligent and resilient. Not diligent like the so called search for bin laden but diligent as in when a cop gets shot. Funny how almost all the cop killers are the subject of a massive nationwide manhunt. And funny how almost all of them get caught. Please understand I do not mean to stir up hurtful and possibly unresolved feelings but I'm confused; when a law enforcement official gets killed in the line of duty and the killer is at large, other law enforcement officials will not stop until they catch the suspected perpetrator. Yet when one asshole, like the one mentioned above gets the blame or recognition for killing a few thousand regular citizens, it becomes a challenge to find him. Hmmm. You must not let yourself be swayed by those with clear consciences and those with strong moral values. People can perfect anything – even if it is immoral. Persistence overcomes resistance.

Chapter Nine
Your Relationship Is What You Say It Is

The problem with most people who cheat besides the fact that they cheat is the fact that they try too hard to cover their indiscretions. They do this by most often making their relationships seem too perfect, when in actuality this is an impossible feat. These people seem to let nothing bother them. They have this feeling of perpetual happiness. Granted sex, especially sex, which is achieved through an adulterous union, will make most people happy. However the automatic change from a person getting mad over his or her significant other smashing the family car to them not raising an eyebrow over the significant other not wanting to have sex for a few weeks at a time, will definitely be noticed. This is the biggest 'dead giveaway' in adulterous unions. If every time a person cheated, they acted differently, how easy would it be to detect infidelity? The thing, which allows people to get caught after committing infidelity is the fact that even though many times they want to cheat, they do not always want to end the relationship. This care factor will cause an individual to take the extra time needed to cover his or her tracks and try to make everything seem as right as possible. This is good but there is such a thing as od-ing or over doing it. People don't always realize how they respond to situations. Quite often they are aware that there is a response but the exact response or the exact level of response is a mystery to everyone except the significant other. It's the same thing as being able to see the forest from the trees. You may not be mad but your partner may assume that you are because of a facial expression that you normally have when you are mad or it just may be your body language, which sends the wrong signal. Sometimes these things are done unwittingly and the bad thing about this is that while you may not notice them, your partner almost assuredly will. This is where our old friend deception comes in to play. A person has to be able to mentally add infidelity to their daily or weekly agenda. It must be added in such a way that it will not cause any deviations whatsoever in that person's life. This is difficult in some respects because most people have what's called a conscience. They cannot knowingly hurt or risk hurting another person for no reason. This is easy in other respects because many people know how to completely ignore their conscience. Don't believe me? Can anyone say pedophile? Yeah I know some people have this theory that child molesters do not intend to hurt children. They just actually love the children they involve themselves with but personally I think that's some bullshit. I may be alone here but I think that somewhere in these sick perverted minds of theirs, there was something saying 'wait a minute Chester, this is wrong – but they went ahead and did whatever it was they did anyway. That's what you call ignoring one's conscience to the extreme.

What people who are trying to excel in the art of infidelity should do is pay attention to what they normally do before committing an indiscretion so that when the time comes for them to potentially break their significant others hearts, they will be ready. During unscripted and unintentional interviews for my books, I have heard countless women speak of how they were always able to tell when their men were cheating because of how different the men would act. This acting different consisted of a multitude of things, the least of which being the famous bringing home of flowers. It is unbelievably sad that infidelity has progressed to such a point where a person cannot even do something nice for his or her significant other anymore because of the stigma or negative connotation associated with it. There was a time not long ago when if a man brought home flowers, the wife or girlfriend was overjoyed. Everybody at the wife or girlfriend's job was jealous beyond belief. Even the female who sold the man the flowers, wished they were for her. Now, all of the above individuals have but one thing on their minds – the belief that that man is a fucking dog and he is trying to make up to his significant other after getting busted in infidelity or trying to sway the significant other's thinking away from the possibility of infidelity. That's why if you bring home flowers once, continue to do it. If you don't normally, don't start. The dreaded change is what always catches people in infidelity situations because change is almost always noticeable. When a woman attempts to change a man from the 'happy go lucky, single, sex with whoever he wants guy' into straight to work, straight to home, one-woman guy, the change is noticeable. Its not always welcome but it is definitely noticeable. If people who were interested in an affair were to take the time to realize that they fight every time the significant other comes home late without calling or argued each time a bill was paid late, they would be fully aware of what to continue to do after an affair so as not to create suspicion. Unfortunately, most times they don't. People usually let infidelity dictate their emotions, meaning if the affair is a good one, they will be happy and carefree in their 'committed relationship.' If the infidelity is not going according to plan, then one of the people involved will unwittingly make things difficult on the home front. Your relationship is what you say it is means if you give your partner and everyone else around no reason to believe the relationship is in jeopardy, they probably never will believe that it is.

    In many instances, it takes a long time to build a reputation. For instance, there is the professional athlete, there is also the seasoned real estate pro and there is even the used car dealer. Out of the three previous examples, the used car salesman is the one, which requires the most amount of time to build a positive reputation because most people in this world have an automatic distrust as well as dislike for salespeople. This is mainly because historically, salespeople have had one thing one thing on their minds at all times and this was nothing more than making the sale. These people did not care too much about feelings, which meant they would pretty much lie to you. These people did not care too much about how you looked in whatever it was they were trying to sell you, which meant they would pretty much lie to you again. These people did not care whether or not you got hurt using whatever it was they tried to sell you, which SURPRISE! pretty much meant they were going to lie to you. Thank goodness all salespeople are not the cold, heartless, conniving bastards one would see at most electronics stores. The real estate pro, often known for embellishing, needs time to build a positive working relationship with his clients so that they can refer him to others. In essence, he too is a salesman but nowhere near the low level of used car sales. The professional athlete is usually in the public eye more than the other two. He is the one who influences generations by doing his job. Remember Michael Jordan? Quite possibly one of the best ball players ever. There was a point in his career when he threw up a basketball, the crowd didn't hope, they knew it was going into the basket. He had achieved that reputation through what I and most of his fans would consider hard and consistent work. Now there are other types of reputations, which can be achieved in a relatively much shorter amount of time. I'm talking about a matter of minutes as opposed to months or years as in the cases above. The most popular type of quick reputation is the one a young lady gets when she has premarital sex or kids out of wedlock. This woman could in fact be the most capable parental figure ever but according to society's beliefs on what a person should and should not do, she will more than likely be considered fast or worst case scenario, a whore. The same type of 'judgment' is found in many relationships because a person is not judged in this world by his or her actions as much as by what others believe his actions to be. There is another famous Michael who has quite a reputation also. Only his is not as stellar as the one mentioned above. I will not focus too much on his reputation but to say that a bit of it deals with his interaction with young people. Many of the people who know of this reputation get their information from the media, hearsay and basically second hand sources. Personally I don't believe many people know what happened but people talk and like magic, a reputation is formed. This is the way a cheater has to make his relationship seem. He must direct the thinking of people – both inside and outside the relationship. Deception toward someone inside a relationship, such as a husband or wife is hard enough but mass deception; the fooling of family, friends and the community at large is what needs to be mastered. It can be accomplished by the way of the professional athlete, real estate pro and used car salesman – trial, error, practice and concentration. Or it can be accomplished by the way of the unwed mother. It must be remembered that people are forming judgments and opinions from the moment they see you. Those judgments and opinions are what you must manipulate. If you always tell everybody you know that you love your wife unconditionally and you hold true to this story, then sooner or later, people will believe it – even if you are just saying it to be saying it. If you have the means and you buy a brand new car with a big red bow sitting on the top of it and have it delivered to your significant other in the middle of the day, so that everybody can see, most of the people, I'm guessing somewhere around ninety percent of those in attendance will believe that you are severely in love and don't really care who knows it. This is how you direct deception. Those groups of people, both the ones you tell you love your significant other everyday and the ones who see the car with the big red bow, will probably never know or never suspect that you have or are contemplating having someone on the side. And the main reason they probably will never suspect you of being the dirty ass, sadistic, low down dog you are is because you have silly puddied their mindset into one, which resembles 'he or she is too good to cheat.' Remember your relationship is what you say it is.

Manipulation is one of the most often used tactics when committing infidelity – next to deception of course. It is often easy to deceive someone but to manipulate sometimes takes a bit more skill. Here's an example of manipulation at work; a man who is interested in a married woman may have attained the level of friend. He may call this woman, even when her significant other is home. He may even ask 'doesn't your man care that I call' to which the woman may respond 'He cares, he just not obsessive.' The interested man may try to manipulate the married woman's thinking into one of non concern on the part of the husband and can most easily do this by using the 'If he really cared, he would monitor or at least restrict the amount of male call traffic' line. People only need a small slice of unproven accusations for them to from enough doubt, which for most is enough to knock them off of their cloud of complacency.

Manipulation can extend to driving one's thought process away from what is actual truth. In an employment situation, where the propensity for relationships or infidelity is usually high, a woman may totally ignore a particular pursuing man. The reason for this attitude is not due to the woman showing her extremely high level of morals or self respect nor is it because there is not the shared

level of interest. It could be the almost never thought of option; maybe the two of them actually already know each other from outside the workplace. Maybe at the workplace, the particular woman has the reputation of saint and letting others at the job know she has screwed this dude, who just may be the biggest male whore at the job may screw up her reputation also. This is exactly the same thing police and other law enforcement agencies do when trying to infiltrate those groups they have a vested interest in shutting down. They will use someone who seems to have the biggest dislike for law enforcement in general. They will not send someone in with the attitude of 'I like the police and the job they do in the community.' They will more than likely use someone who openly expresses attitudes resembling 'fuck those blue uniform wearing, minority men harassing, civil rights violating, cock sucking bastards!'
(Oh just to be clear, I don't really dislike law enforcement and related organizations, I am just using this example for dramatic effect!) lol.
Continuing along the lines of manipulation, there is a big misconception regarding lawyers. Lawyers are not here to defend you as many people think, lawyers are put in place to represent you. Defending a person is protecting that person from attack, harm or danger or speaking on behalf of an accused person in

court. Lawyers represent people because people are unable to represent themselves in the right manner. I like to believe that many lawyers are not that much smarter than anybody else, just differently educated. They are educated in the art of manipulation. Their jobs are basically to manipulate the beliefs of others. The one who does it the best is the winner. This is one of the many things cheaters do to achieve their goal of infidelity. A cheater will manipulate a person's thinking so that the intended target (person the cheater wants to sleep with) will believe the significant other is doing something wrong or if not doing something wrong, then acting in a way which will make the target believe there are other reasons for the significant other acting the way he or she is. These cheater lawyers represent if you will, the target in that they will take the significant other's or defendants words and actions and twist then twist them around so that the target will be inclined to believe other than what actually exists. There is a certain mindset, which these cheater lawyers seek out. It is the one of 'he or she is just being nice.' These cheater lawyers will find someone who looks for the good in people and manipulate their minds like silly puddy. The significant others in these relationships who can see what's being done long before infidelity happens are often hit by the target with accusations of 'you're just jealous and or insecure.' Then, when the cheater lawyer wins the case and has sex with the target and the significant other says 'I told you this would happen' the target will most often respond with 'I wanted it to happen' and the reason he or she will say this is to save face – to be able to show they were not played or manipulated.

Chapter Ten
Ramifications

Here's a quiz: What is the quickest way to stop a perpetual speeder? Answer: an accident. What is the quickest way to stop a perpetual cheater? Answer: getting caught. What is the quickest way to stop many happy relationships? Answer: a baby. Everything we do in life has consequences or ramifications. The more painful the ramifications are, the more likely the lesson is going to be remembered. As in the previous examples, the actions, which caused the usually abrupt change in a person's behavior were severe enough to either make that person really reevaluate his or her reasons for doing or serious enough to end that person's life. When it comes to infidelity, the potential ramifications can stretch from one end of the spectrum to the other. A person can lose the relationship they are presently in or he or she can lose a life. In this day and age, far too many people still try and downplay the seriousness of an affair. In some Middle Eastern countries, if a person is caught stealing, the thief's hand is cut off. Sounds severe? Well imagine losing one's penis for having an orgasm. At the time of this line being written, the year is 2010 and the world is consistently changing. Technology it seems; is changing every single minute – forget about every day. The only thing, which has not or does not change, is the fact that people are crazy. People have been, are and will probably until the end of time continue to be crazy. (Throwing babies out the window and shit like that) Where's the logic? Being a NY native, it's hard to find anything that would make me raise an eyebrow about it's originality but the killing; especially the killing over infidelity always seems to astound. When I started The Correct Way To Fool Around series, the basis behind it was not so that people could cheat on each other like undisciplined teenagers; it was so that people would know what to look out for if they suspected someone they were involved with of cheating. (Whether any of you believe that or not) That way, they would know what steps to take to counteract the potential infidelity, meaning they would know how to throw a monkey wrench in the cheating partner's plans before the plan actually had a chance to materialize. I know that every single person who purchased my books did not have positive intentions regarding the enclosed content and for those people maybe, hopefully they got some positive assistance from them. I'm not mad at them, I am not a judge of their character nor do I have to deal with their crisis of conscience. Aside from what's above, one of my not so positive reasons for writing these books were so that if people were actually going to use my books as reference material for the act of infidelity, then maybe they could have an affair without actually getting killed. You see, even in our unbelievably super advanced, technological day and age, many people are stupid. Okay, maybe stupid is a bit harsh but I believe many of us are completely heartless when it comes to the keeping secret of an affair. These people will be so blatant in their activities that Helen Keller would be able to see them. And she's blind – and dead. I call these people heartless because they don't even have the slightest level of common decency to at least try to hide an indiscretion. It's almost like they're saying 'hey honey, look at me! I'm about to insert my penis into another woman! Don't blink, you might miss it! These, in my opinion are the really stupid ones. They cheat with no type of discretion what so ever, then when they get caught, wonder why the significant other one day flips out and tries to rip off the person's penis. I know cheating is wrong. Even though the majority of the material I write deals with the day to day operations of infidelity and how to circumvent the possibility of getting caught, I am willing to bet that the majority of the people in this world would rather be kept in the dark about a partner's misgivings than have that partner come clean about sleeping around with whoever. I know also that many people will disagree with me because they feel that even though ignorance is bliss, truth is everlasting. This is good and all but I wish for one second that these truth seekers and truth lovers imagine how they would feel if they find themselves involved with a sex addict. Would these people be so accepting if everyday or every week their significant other came home and said honey, in the spirit of truth and happiness, I have to tell you I had sex with somebody new…again? I don't think so. Infidelity is a fun but dangerous game. It is kinda like that Russian game where a person puts one bullet in the chamber of a six or seven chamber revolver, then spins the chamber and points the gun at his head, then pulls the trigger. That game is fun only if you win. And just like infidelity, if you do get away with murder, so to speak, it will be something you can brag about forever (to certain people, of course). If you do not win or get away with it, then just like the game with the gun, the consequences will be deadly or if not deadly, then disastrous.

When it comes to ramifications, one of the things people do is spend far too much time thinking of ways to get even with a lover who has spurned them. I'm not saying it shouldn't be done because an eye for an eye is how most of the people in our society live but the ways in which people do things is often unnecessary. I've noticed how some people will call their friends and family to get ideas on how to get even with another. People will watch made for television movies based on infidelity to get an idea of how to get even. People will even seek out the assistance of a contract killer to avenge a broken heart. All of the above methods can seem more than justified to the person who has had his or her heart broken but almost all of them come with unpleasant consequences. There is one often overlooked solution for vengeance regarding infidelity and that is the task of doing absolutely nothing. I know many of you are asking what type of vengeance is that but many of you do not realize how powerful the mind actually is. Think about this; a person who gets caught cheating is guilty. If the couple stays together, that guilt will stay with that guilty person. Now combine that with the mind's absolutely miraculous wondering capabilities. A guilty person who cares about his or her significant other will have no idea what is on the mind of the innocent partner. He or she will not know if the partner is planning to leave him or her. He will not know if the innocent party is planning to cheat. He will not even know if the innocent party is planning to do him harm. All the innocent party has to do is smile as if nothing has bothered him. This will drive the guilty party insane because most people know that any action will cause a reaction. Most reactions are outward. When a person holds things in, as history has shown, they will usually come out in one form or another. A guilty person waiting for a reaction from someone he has harmed is about the same as a guilty person waiting for a sentence from a judge. That person will have no idea what reaction will emerge or in what form. This will give the innocent party free will to do whatever he or she wants and depending on the nature of this person or depending upon how bad they were hurt, this person can make the guilty party pay for the rest of his or her life. To add insult to injury, if the guilty party were to ever complain about the treatment or should I say ill-treatment he or she receives, all the innocent party would have to do is mention those famous six words; I'm not the one who cheated!

As stated before, when people cheat on others, often the damage they cause can travel from one end of the spectrum to the other. An affair can cause the innocent party to constantly relive the pain, which was suffered by the cheating spouse over and over. An affair can cause physical, as well as emotional pain to the innocent victim. It can make a person emotionally unavailable to anybody else who finds interest in him or her. It causes a person to reevaluate himself or herself as a person. It can cause them to start to wonder 'is there something wrong with me?' They wonder if they can exist with this person who has dashed their hopes and dreams of perpetual happiness while not completely sure if they can trust him or her ever again. They wonder if anybody or everybody else they ever deal with will cheat on them as well.

One of the more unpleasant ramifications regarding infidelity is the possibility that one or more of the women a person happens to be sleeping with may just become pregnant. This by itself is bad enough but is pales in comparison to the trifling bitch blackmailing the individual who got her that way. There's a popular saying, which goes hell hath no fury like a woman scorned. Okay that philosophy is kinda understandable but some of these women feel as if it's their right to make a man pay for his mistakes or indiscretions for all eternity. Some women while involved in an affair, may become pregnant and request some money from the man to help with pro choice methods. Other women may try and milk this man for all they can and by this I mean requesting, better yet ordering that man to pay what's called hush money to the woman every so often. This hush money is given to the woman who gets pregnant so that she may 1) choose not to have the child and 2) keep quiet about ever being pregnant in the first place – as well as about the affair in general. This will put the man in a not so good position because after giving the mistress the hush money, she could violate the agreement by having the child and by letting the wife know. If the mistress decides to be nice and not tell, the man will still have to find a way to support his family on whatever the mistress <u>allows</u> him to have after she gets her cut. And we all know what happens then; the wife in her infinite wisdom, sooner or later will begin to inquire of the husband 'so what happened to all your money?' This is how people often get hurt or worse in infidelity situations. They keep secrets and not only do they keep secrets, they expect others to keep those secrets as well. People usually only keep secrets if they benefit themselves. If however there is the potential for monetary or personal gain, more than likely that secret is going to the highest bidder. People, both men and women use disposable sex partners for just this reason. By disposable I mean those sex partners who either sell sex in strip clubs or who are employed as escorts or streetwalkers. These people are in the business of having sex – nothing more. So there is very little chance if any at all of there being any kind of connection to them whatsoever. Often the conversation between the disposable sex partner and the married person entails very little more than 'how much?' and 'how long?' and if God forbid, the female disposable sex partner were to ever become pregnant, it would be up to her to either use a pro choice method or have the child. Whatever the case the married individual having the affair would never know or be responsible.

Chapter Eleven
Possessions

When it comes to the reasons behind why infidelity is committed at such an astounding rate, there are many often known and overlooked causes. One of those known yet overlooked causes is the difference in how a person is treated while in a relationship. When most people are questioned about what it takes to keep a relationship afloat, the vast majority of them will answer with the following: honesty, trustworthiness, loyalty and dependability. Granted, these are some of the ingredients necessary for a relationship's longevity but they are by no means all. One of the ingredients consistently left out of the happiness 'stew' is fairness. People expect to be treated fairly but far too few of them actually work at it. For some reason or other people feel that fairness is a birthright. They feel that everyone is automatically going to threat them as equals just because they have the ability to breathe. This belief is wrong. People often feel that life is about looking out for number one – or I got mine, you get yours.' People also feel that a person can have anything they want in this world just as long as what they want does not interfere with whatever somebody else owns. Why is it for instance that a person can beat the shit out of their kids without feeling any type of remorse or concern but will lose their fucking mind when someone else does or even attempts to? Why is it that people only seem to care about car theft when it happens to them? Quite often it is because these people feel that someone has violated them or their 'space.' Child abuse as I'm sure most of us will agree is wrong but many abusers don't see it that way. Hell, many of them don't even see themselves as abusers. Most of them feel that 'hey this child belongs to me so I can do whatever I please, whenever and wherever I feel like doing it.' The same feeling exists in many relationships. People can be in relationships, which are so stagnant that moss could actually grow underneath the feet of the people involved but will only get mad or concerned when someone threatens the relationship's existence. Many times infidelity is viewed as a personal attack on the innocent party in the relationship. Think about something, when a person gets caught cheating, how often is there sympathy for that individual as opposed as anger and blame toward that individual? Not much. People are very quick to say 'you hurt me' instead of 'you have a problem and I want to understand' or let's see how we can help you correct your problem or maybe even 'there's a problem with us — let's work together to try and fix it.' Many times people in relationships believe that the relationship is all about them. What the other party in the relationship desires is secondary. When a person views his or her mate as property, he or she will treat that person as such. Infidelity can easily infect a union of this sort because all someone outside of the relationship will have to do is treat the property owners property like a human being and problem solved. Relationships are not hard. People in relationships make them hard. What must be remembered is that there are basic rules, which apply to all relationships and one of those basic rules is to keep or at least attempt to keep each other happy. I can think of no simpler way to begin to accomplish this than to treat each other as equals but that's easier said than done. Many people in relationships misconstrue the meaning of the word relationship. Quite often instead of each person in the relationship being able to say 'I am my own person. I have my own life but I am willing to share it with you.' These people say something to the effect of 'you are mine and everything you have is mine. This includes your property, thoughts and feelings. I know this sounds ludicrous, especially when one says it out loud but there are many relationships out here, which follow this exact blueprint. People are so controlling and sometimes so unwittingly so that they actually force their mates into the arms of someone else. I also understand how this can happen because almost everybody in a relationship wants to control his or her partner's heart. They want their partner to never be emotionally or physically attracted to anybody else. The unfortunate thing about this is that no one can reasonably expect this to happen. One of the biggest things about relationships, which cause turmoil, is the feeling of being claustrophobic. This is basically a feeling of being unpleasantly or uncomfortably confined. This boxed in feeling will cause a person to long for freedom or independence. As almost any person who has initiated, been a part of and or survived an affair will probably tell you, infidelity gives a person good feeling. When I speak of good feeling, I am doing so under the assumption that the affair ended on a good note, meaning nobody was hurt physically or emotionally and the original relationship (the one before the affair) is still intact. This good feeling can come in a number of ways, for instance; it could come from knowledge of the fact that a person has actually gotten away with doing something, which is looked upon as taboo in most relationships. It could also come from the feeling that the person gets from the actual physical part of the affair as in his or her body <u>feels</u> good to me whenever we do it. Whatever the case, infidelity offers a type of freedom from that boxed in, uncomfortable feeling. When a person feels they own something or someone, even if he or she does not verbalize it, the feeling of subservience will be present. This feeling will often bring out a feeling on the part of the person who is quote unquote owned. That feeling will resemble a feeling of 'you don't own me and to prove that you don't own me I will do something to prove my independence!' This is a kind of acting out people do which is similar in many ways to teenagers and their need for expression.

People will have sex with others and not just a couple of others but many others just to prove their position. Many people don't believe that their partners are equal to them and this can be due to one partner making more money than the other or it could be due to one partner being a woman - whatever the case, that belief will cause problems. At the very least it will cause infidelity. On the opposite end of the spectrum it can cause the destruction of a relationship. Being possessive in a relationship is the same as being unwilling to relinquish control. A person who is not willing to give up control will not be able to completely give up his or her heart – in other words he or she will not allow themselves to be vulnerable. This is bad because vulnerability is part of most relationships. Vulnerability is part of being in love. Let's stop for a minute and imagine a hypothetical situation where everybody thought of his or her partners as complete equals – where there was no possessiveness or jealousy. This world would be absolutely wonderful. There would be no scheming, no hiding of emotions, no wondering if the other is actually as much in love as his partner is. Unfortunately the world is not that way. People have been hurt before. People keep their feelings hidden because they fear being hurt again. I do not mean to say that people who are possessive are not cheaters, because everybody is capable of cheating. What I do believe is that the people who are involved with those who are possessive in nature are more inclined to cheat because of that fact. (but then again could be rambling).

Being possessive is not a bad thing. Wait let me rephrase that. Being possessive is not a bad thing unless it is in family or in one on one relationships. Think about something; possessive people often become overprotective parents. Overprotective parents often have kids who run away. Overprotective or possessive people in relationships often have partners who run away, so to speak. People have to remember that a person cannot be controlled. That is imprisonment. That is jail. A person must be free to choose the life he or she wants to live. A person cannot be controlled, neither can a person's heart – although it is a nice fantasy.

Chapter Twelve
Complacency

There are many people in this world who believe that all relationships go through phases. The number of phases, just like the reasons behind infidelity, can stretch from one end of the spectrum to the other. The most popular relationship phases I have encountered are infatuation, getting to know, love and complacency. Most people already know about what's entailed in the lustful infatuation stage; this is the stage where the very sight of him or her turns you on, where the thought of this person makes you feel like a school child beaming with joy – and let's not forget the sex. The infatuation stage is for some the best part of the relationship due to the sometimes massive amounts of physical intimacy. What often comes next is the getting to know a person stage. This involves finding out a person's likes and dislikes, habits and quirks and deciding whether or not you can tolerate them. The getting to know stage also involves family and friends. Many people still don't believe that a relationship never only involves two people. A relationship can include but is not limited to: best friends, parents, psychics, former lovers, dogs, cats, the penal system, psychiatrists and even children. When in the getting to know stage, a person must skillfully merge everyone associated with himself into the life of the person he is dealing with. Then comes for many, the best part of the relationship phases, love. Love is considered the culmination of the previous two, infatuation and getting to know somebody. Love is when a couple can settle comfortably into their prospective roles as husband and wife or boyfriend and girlfriend or whatever. The complacency stage is the last and I believe the most dangerous because that is the stage when infidelity most often sneaks into a relationship. When complacency sets in, people in relationships feel as though they have reached a level that no longer requires work. They feel that the relationship is fine and as long as neither party does anything to upset the delicate balance that they have achieved, the relationship will be fine for the rest of eternity. This is a common feeling. It is common because more people would rather sit back and have their relationships work for them than to consistently work on the relationship to make sure it's going the way the two of them desire. When complacency settles on the part of one, often it comes along with the belief that the other is too set in his or her ways to deviate from the pattern, which is his or her life. People in the complacency phase believe they know their partners better than their partners know themselves. They believe that any thoughts or desires a partner may have regarding the opposite sex are nothing more than thoughts and desires because to act on them would be a relationship threatening act that the other would not dare – and this is because the other partner again knows him or her so well. But this is the trick that complacency holds for those caught in its grip. It will massage the mind of a person so well that that person will believe that his or her significant other is no longer capable of doing something wrong. And at that precise moment, infidelity will swoop down on the relationship the way a bald eagle would when attempting to secure a mackerel from shallow waters. Infidelity, with all of its strong points and acquaintances, will lean on complacency because complacency is a state of mind. It is a state of mind, which can be manipulated by people believing it can never exist. There is a common saying, which states that the greatest illusion the devil ever performed was convincing the world he does not exist. It is the same thing with complacency. If a person is so comfortable in his or her relationship, that the thought of infidelity is never allowed to enter into that person's mind, how hard would it be for the other partner to commit it? I'm guessing not hard at all. Complacency in my opinion can best be described as the extreme softening of one's defenses or the dumbing down of logic. If a couple is diligent in their beliefs and by diligent I mean always aware of the possibility of infidelity intruding on their relationship, it will be that much harder for infidelity to actually do it. This goes back to one of the basic necessities for happiness in relationships and that basic necessity is communication. The problem with communication is that it is not always ongoing. It can wane. When the communication breakdown occurs, people in relationships often assume things about one another as well as the relationship. These relationship assumptions are the first steps in a relationship becoming complacent. Now in most aspects of life, complacency is not such a bad thing because as stated before, it's common – and it's common because people have a need for constant reinvention. The problem with most people's need for constant reinvention is the fact that most people never achieve it. They get bored. Think about it; people get bored with shoes because they go out of style. People get bored with their jobs because they become monotonous. People get bored with their cars because new ones come out every year and finally, people get bored with their lives because they find themselves falling into ruts. These are common things because we as human beings are taught from a very young age that variety is what keeps life interesting and is what is necessary for a happy existence. One way this is taught is by the massive amount of toys some children are given each and every year at Christmas. If variety were not such a big deal, one or two toys would be more than sufficient. The only problem with this philosophy is that most people are creatures of comfort. They know full well what is good for them yet they will insist upon things, which make themselves feel good. Now as a parent I understand fully how annoying a screaming child can sometimes be and I also understand the temptation to give in and cater to the child's demands in return for a little peace and quiet. But what this does is start the child on a possibly never ending road to expectation. The thing that many people in this world know but refuse to actually focus on is the fact that all adults start out as children. If there is uncorrected behavior in a child, ten times out of ten, that uncorrected behavior will carry over into adulthood. Now this is not to say that having a small selection of toys as a child is wrong, it just promotes a certain way of thinking later on in life. Many people expose their children to as much as humanly possible; meaning toys, clothes, books, and cars – you name it. But when it comes to relationships, these children with the 'I can have anything I want' mindset who grow into adults are expected to limit their choices to one. Doesn't seem easy or feasible for that matter, does it? Complacency can exist in every aspect of a person's life. The only place complacency is not well tolerated is in relationships. You see people can live with a boring job, why, because that boring job provides benefits, the most important benefit being the ability to live. People can live with a boring pair of shoes, why, because it provides benefits also; the most important benefit being protection of one's feet. We desire style but we can live without it. People can live with the same car, year after year and why, because it provides the most important benefit of getting us from point a to point b. Sure most people would like to drive around in a brand new car if the finances permit but many more people would rather drive around in an old car than not to be able to at all. Relationships are the exception. People will damn near tolerate boredom or complacency in any part of their lives except for their relationships. The difference with the other aspects of people's lives is that when complacency sets in, depending upon how important it is to you, it can be changed in a heartbeat. Job got you to the point where you just want to bite your nails off, swallow them, shit them out, glue them back on then repeat the process? Get a new job. Car makes you so sick at the sight of it that you would rather play Fred Flintstone and ride a dinosaur to work? Get a new one. Footwear so old that the heel has become part of the sole? Buy a new pair of shoes! It's really simplistic. The problem with relationships is that you can't just up and leave when they get boring or complacent. People <u>have</u> to find ways to reinvent the happiness they once had otherwise they become miserable. And what happens when a person in a relationship becomes miserable? That person's actions, whether consciously or not will cause the other person to become miserable. Think about it – ever see a couple where one person does not talk to the other? What happens? The communication is broken; assumptions are made based on the broken communication and each member in the relationship acts on those assumptions. This is how cheating can so easily infect a relationship. People still refuse to believe that a relationship is much like a child in the sense that it needs to be nurtured and taken care of basically for life. The moment that the relationship is left to fend for itself, it becomes complacent. Infidelity, in a way, keeps a relationship new because it often provides the spark needed to jumpstart a stagnating relationship. The problem with infidelity is that it is often like a drug. One time may not be enough. One time may be addicting. That one time spark may end up being a lifelong inferno. Now I am not about to get into that bs debate that so many people these days get into about whether or not cheating is or can be an actual addiction or whether or not there is actually evidence to suggest that the so called cheating gene has any bearing on a person's sexual exploits or decisions. This is because my position is simple; everything in this world can become addicting. People don't like to believe when I say this but there are some urges in this world that a person cannot fight alone. Yea I know that there are some of you reading this who are quick to say that any addiction can be overcome by just a little faith or a little prayer in a chosen higher power or like one former president's wife said, just say no. Okay that's fine and all but what happens when a person does not have that little bit of faith? What happens when a person is not that strong? What happens when a person takes so many drugs that the urge compels her to attempt to sell her own child? What happens when the urge for a drug is so strong that a woman will sell her own body to somebody that she has never seen before and to somebody who she doesn't know if he has any or every disease imaginable? This is just an inkling of the power that some urges possess – and no, a person cannot after being controlled by these types of urges just turn around and just say no. Sometimes the urge for sexual gratification is equivalent to the ones described above. Sometimes a person cannot shut off the urge for sexual gratification once it has been awakened because everybody in this world does not respond to impulses and urges the same way. So yes in my opinion people can be addicted to sex. Trust me.

Another downside to receiving that much needed jumpstart is that aside from having to battle your conscience if you do in fact get away with your indiscretion, is the fact that you might not get away at all and then you will have to explain why you decided to mess around in the first place. Now if this particular stage is reached and you get caught cheating, whether by actually getting caught with your pants down or by your own admission, you may be persuaded into thinking that any ole lie or excuse will suffice. Don't be fooled. This is one of those situations where the tactful truth is essential – not regular truth but truth with extreme tactfulness.

Regular truth is 'I'm bored with you, I'm bored with the relationship, you do nothing that I find interesting – that's why I cheated!' Tactful truth is 'Honey, I'm at a point in my life where I feel I don't know how to make you happy anymore. The person I had the affair with not completely understood me but took the time to try.' Of course if you don't get killed and the person you cheated on is willing to try and work things out, the obvious response will be 'well why didn't you come and talk to me earlier if you were having these feelings?' to which the appropriate comeback will be 'we never communicate, how could I talk to you?' You see if there were actual and ongoing communication, complacency would stand very little chance at becoming a part of that relationship in the first place. Infidelity is something which <u>can</u> be overcome but to have a real or actual chance at doing so, people need to be proactive as in 'let's talk about our relationship and let's talk about it often – let's talk about where it's going and where we want it to go' instead of reactive as in 'you cheated on me and it hurt, now let's see if we can work on our relationship so that we can get it to the point of where it used to be.'

Being proactive means discussing the issue before it has a chance to become a problem. Being reactive means trying to find a solution to a problem, which should have been solved when it was still an issue.

Chapter Thirteen
The Contradictory Nature Of Relationships

There are many things in this world, which are total contradictions. The idea behind many relationships is one of the most popular. Many people will tell you that a healthy relationship is supposed to contain one, if not all of the following: total honesty, fidelity, communication, etc. Those people are full of shit. Relationships are full of deception, ongoing trickery and the occasional outright lie. Every single person walking the face of this earth knows that there is no place for total honesty in a relationship – even though it is necessary for a true relationship. Total honesty entails a person telling the other 'I don't find you attractive anymore' or 'Having sex with you is boring' when the situation so calls for that type of truthfulness. The problem with many relationships is that instead of having truth, people desire happiness. It's extremely hard to have both. Complete fidelity, although much desired, cannot truly be expected by anyone because it is not the way most people are raised. People are generally raised to seek out and obtain happiness and wealth or if not actually obtaining happiness and wealth, then getting as close to it as humanly possible. If you really think about it, how often does one really hear a child being taught 'grow up and be faithful to your chosen partner at all costs' as opposed to 'grow up and make lots of money so you can be happy?' With the exception of religious folks, the answer is not very often. What too many people do is equate money and sex with happiness - Always have, always will. Here's proof: If the amount of money a person receives does not make him or her happy, nine times out of ten, said person will do what is necessary to achieve the amount of money which will make him or her happy. Why is it that an extremely low number of people get one job and stay at that job until retirement age? Chances are its because that job does not always completely satisfy a person's needs and or desires. The same thing holds true for sex. Now while it is well understood that there are many reasons people indulge in the act of intercourse, for instance, kids, money, status and compulsion, the most recognized reason is that of enjoyment. Many people are still attending this illusion institution, which has them believing that one; sex means the same thing to one party as it does to the other and two; sex is the highest expression of a couple's love, instead of the end of a drunken night of serial porn watching. Many people get involved in a relationship based on how good the sex is. If the sex wanes for any reason, the relationship is over.

Communication is a double edged sword – in many instances it means a person is damned if they do and damned if they don't. Communication entails, among many other things, talking and talking has a first cousin whose name is understanding. Many in relationships talk to each other but don't always understand what the other is trying to get across to them. They hear but don't listen, so to speak. This can come across by many different reasons – the person attempting to get his point across could be inefficient at expressing himself or the person attempting to understand the point could just be a total fucking retard. Many times, people don't want to hear what's being said because they do not believe the person speaking is intelligent enough to be giving advice at all and this is a bad thing because in a relationship, if one does not respect the views, opinions and advice of the person he or she is involved with, what's the real point of the relationship? In any case this causes miscommunication, which causes problems in the relationship. There are other things such as the outright lies and deception, which are necessary for a relationship's existence. These come about because although they may be morally wrong, they often protect the level of happiness in most relationships. Think about that for a second and ask yourself, have you or anybody you know ever been involved with a very jealous individual and at one time or another had someone approach you or someone you know with feelings of amour and you did not inform your significant other? Of course you have – everybody has. The reason why most people do not inform the significant other is because the significant other is one; jealous, two; violent or three; jealous and violent. Fuck all the nonsense about truthfulness and having no secrets between one another, if a person fears for his or her life, that person will do or not do whatever is necessary to avoid harm to him or herself.

People always have and always will dictate what another person's relationship is going to be. Many times people do this intentionally. Many times they do it subconsciously. Sometimes it's even done indirectly. The fact that people almost always want to make themselves seem better than someone else is what causes a relationship's direction or misdirection. For instance, one woman in a relationship may say to her best friend who is not in a relationship ' I make my husband do this and that and I dare him to complain!' If the unmarried woman never views the husband as unhappy in his relationship, she will most likely believe that he is in fact either happy or a total wuss. If she believes the latter, chances are very well that when this woman becomes involved in a relationship, she will try said conditioning techniques on the one she becomes involved with. For some reason or other, people still believe that what they see can be easily duplicated if they do exactly what they see being done. These people do not realize that happiness, just like complacency in a relationship takes time. What works for the lady above could in fact get her best friend killed, assaulted or left alone if the best friend were to attempt it without months and perhaps years of getting to know the one she is involved with. People outside of a relationship will always assume they know what is going on inside of someone else's relationship just by what they see when that couple is together. People will assume more if they hear things from one or both of the parties in the relationship. But it should be stated that this is never a completely reliable screening method in determining whether a couple is happy, sad or whatever else. Reason being, couples use deception all the time. It could be toward each other or toward the public at large. If it's toward the public at large, it could be because the couple desires little or no interaction from outside, so they will say things to the effect of 'I love my wife' or 'I love my husband to death' when the exact opposite is possible. If the deception is toward each other, it most often is because one or each person in the relationship desires happiness – and as we all know, happiness can never come from being completely truthful – all the time. I know there are many people who believe only in truth who are just waiting to argue that statement about happiness never being able to come from complete truthfulness and they are well justified in their beliefs but I wish for one second these people would look at relationships in general. If they did, there's a pretty good chance they would see that being completely truthful all the time is guaranteed to cause some sort of unhappiness – even if only for a short period of time. I'm well aware of the 'if you tell one lie, soon you will have to back it up with another and another and soon the back up lies will steamroll out of control causing more detriment than if a person had originally told the truth' thing but just think for a second, what if the lie you told saved someone's life? How many people would be mad at you? I'm guessing not many. I have this conversation more times than I would really like to with those perpetual truth seeking, truth lovers out there who say they would never allow themselves to be put in a position where they would be forced to lie. That sounds good and all but what these people don't seem to understand is that sometimes there will be instances that are beyond a person's ability to control. Here's a not too far out for instance; let's say person A was close friends with an extreme hothead who we'll call person B. Let's say person B was involved with a very attractive girl called person C. Person B never trusted person C. Person B also has an unlicensed gun and person B suspects for whatever reason that his girlfriend person C is being unfaithful. Person B's suspicions turn into accusations and person C turns to her best friend, person D for support. Person B notices the two of them together and decides to take his unlicensed gun over to person C's home to rectify the problem but on the way to commit homicide he runs into person A who by chance just happens to be friends with all of the above. Person B asks person a if he has any knowledge of an affair between person's C and D because he is on the way to kill them. If person A knows for a fact that person's C and D are screwing, and he divulges this to person B, chances are he might quite possibly become an unintentional accomplice. If on the other hand, person A tells person B something to the effect of 'no she is not cheating on you' and this temporarily calms person B down just enough that person A could call person C and warn her or at least slow down person B long enough to call the police and have them arrest person B and his crazy ass, would that be totally wrong? People I have this conversation with often tell me that person B in his state of mind will probably do whatever he has his mind set on doing regardless to whatever person A was to tell him but my thing is if the police can stop this fool and put him away for a few years or if person C and D could know to be on the lookout for this person, then wouldn't that be beneficial to all – even if only temporarily. I understand that lying is morally incorrect but I also understand that most will agree that as morally incorrect as it may be, it _is_ sometimes appropriate. Sometimes people in relationships do not want to upset the bliss that ignorance to certain facts can bring. Sometimes people in relationships do not want to hear that you find someone else more attractive than the man or woman you married. Sometimes people in relationships don't want to hear that maybe the person they love with all their heart does not love them anymore. Complete truthfulness is at the very least, a challenge. It is contradictory because historically, men for the most part believe that an occasional fib will help protect the feelings of the significant other. Women on the other hand usually believe that they can always handle complete truth. They can't. People say that in the long run, complete truthfulness will make for a better and possibly stronger relationship and I am inclined to agree somewhat but a relationship is also about the present. It is often about the happiness a person can bring to another in the here and now. Everybody knows that truth will make for a better 'later on down the line' but if some people are always crushed by the harsh reality of brutal honesty will these people have enough resilience to actually make it to 'later on down the line?' Something to think about.

When it comes to relationships men have a certain way of thinking, as do women. This is not a problem. The problem sets in when one or both parties attempt to have the person they are involved with change his or her thinking to resemble that of the other. Many people don't want to understand that while opposites attract, the fact that people have differences of opinions, among other things is what helps to keep the relationship interesting – not to mention keeping the relationship from becoming complacent. On the other hand being too opposite will cause problems as well because people must have a common ground on which they can communicate. Men and women both envision what a relationship should entail and almost 100% percent of the time the envisioning views are wrong – okay maybe not wrong but not exactly what the other gender would completely agree upon. In relationships, there must always be a level of moderation and adjustment because people will never be exactly how someone else wants them to be and neither will their thinking. This fact by itself causes people to initially be at odds. What helps the situation is the fact that couples are usually willing to work together to find that necessary common ground which will make the differences in opinions and methods of thinking little more than each person's individuality. The best example I know of about the contradictory nature of relationships is the misunderstandings of infidelity. Many times people give the title infidelity to situations, which are nothing more than miscommunications. People don't always verbalize what they want in regard to certain relationships. They expect the person they get involved with to automatically know and cooperate without deviation. Here's a for instance; a couple gets together and by together I mean committed dating but no sex. The woman mentioning that she never has sex with someone she is dating until after at least a year of togetherness implies the committed part. The man whom this woman is involved with never verbally agrees but accepts the relationship by not disagreeing. After a few months the woman catches the man with another woman. She flips out, ostracizes the man from her life, tells her girlfriends how right they were and hates men for all eternity. Now, is the woman right for being upset? Of course she is. However she must be partially faulted for assuming and not confirming that the desire for the relationship or the terms of such was equal to hers. Many times in relationships people have their own selfish agendas. This is not a gender thing – men and women do it. No matter how much you love them, no matter how much you say you'll never leave them, no matter how much you do for them; it's possible that they could only be in the relationship for convenience. In the not so fictional example above, the woman already had in her mind what she wanted and expected from her relationship. This on the one hand is good but on the other can be potentially dangerous because while a person should have a certain plan for how he or she wants his or her life to turn out, that person should not have tunnel vision in regard to everything else. Some people focus so hard on having their lives turn out precisely the way they envision that they don't completely notice that the person they are involved with really doesn't give two shits. The guy in the above example could well be someone who really doesn't care about the woman and her one year – no sex rule or he could be one of those people who just needs a little more time than most to fully commit himself to a relationship. It's not always about a person wanting to commit infidelity; sometimes it's about knowing what infidelity actually is. Sometimes it's about being on the same level as the person you are boinking and sometimes it's about total honesty with regard to feelings as well as simple communication.

Chapter Fourteen
More Deception

In one of my prior works, I mentioned how it would not be totally impossible for a high school dropout to maintain a successful relationship with a college graduate. Many people have questioned my reasoning behind this statement. Let me explain. For some reason or other, many people believe that education is the only common ground necessary or if not the only, then the main common ground necessary to facilitate a successful relationship. This is misconception. Now while using one's education in daily life is a necessity, having the same level of education as the person one is involved in a relationship with is not. A person could have graduated from college with a baccalaureate but have no idea at all on the correct way or the most accepted way to raise a happy and productive child. On the other hand, a person who has dropped out of school may have been bestowed with the honor of early parenting and have gained enough knowledge to rival certain teachers of childcare. For this type of relationship to occur, the two individuals would have to share a level of compatibility, which extends way past academics. What people don't always like to accept is the fact that there are many compatibility levels, which draw people to one another. People can be compatible based on thinking patterns, sex patterns, likes, dislikes, biases and a host of other criteria but the problem with many folks is that they share what I like to call a closed minded mentality. The thought process of these people resemble 'they're both the same race, so they're compatible' or 'they're both rich, so they're again compatible.' What many do not realize is that two people could be of the same race and in the same income bracket yet have nothing else in common other than those two things. Many people in our society mistakenly label or judge others by their accomplishments in life, for instance; a person graduates from college – wham bam they're smart. A person drops out of high school – it's because he or she is not intelligent enough to finish. What people also don't like to acknowledge is the fact that everybody has a certain level of intelligence. That level however is not always displayed at all times nor is it dictated by traditional educational standards. Personally I am a gigantic fan of deception. One of the things people who share my love of deception often do is extract pity and sympathy from others. This is most often done by a person acting as if they have difficulty understanding simple things or by a person acting as if he or she has no fucking conceptual idea of what is going on around them. There is a particular practice, which I love and one that I notice quite often and this is what people do at a new job. People will act like they do not know how to do something the job entails if that particular thing entails too much work. Instead of a person saying 'I don't want to do all of this work (which will most likely get him or her fired) that person will mess up the task put before him. But notice the person will not mess up the job irreparably – only enough so that others will conclude 'he can't do this job, let's give him something easy.' (Which is what the individual wanted all along.) Many people think that if a person screws up something, totally or otherwise, it is because that person knows no better. This is the power of deception. When people offer resumes, which put their occupational knowledge at a 90th or better percentile, then when hired cannot do the job, it's not always because the resume was doctored. Often it's because these people are lazy or because they don't feel the payment is commensurate with the effort.

Now on the other hand there are some people who are just blinking retarded. Don't pass judgment; I'm not being mean. I call these people blinking retarded because they are the ones who drop out of school and not due to family constraints or work commitments but due to the fact that they need extensive remedial help but yet and still think they are as smart as everybody else. Some of these blinking retarded people cannot understand many of the things that go on in life, as well as in relationships as well as or on the same level as the people they get involved with. This causes problems in relationships because many people get involved with others for if not the wrong reasons, then reasons which defy all logical understanding. If a person who is blinking retarded is involved in a relationship but yet does not know or is not capable of understanding what typically goes on in a 'normal' relationship, said relationship will cause the couple to be at constant odds. I regrettably have been in a couple of these types of relationships and have experienced many more and the one thing I consistently notice is that those who are deemed blinking retarded do not seem to want to help themselves do any better. It's as if they feel 'I'm just as smart as everybody else so I don't need to learn anything.' That type of thinking is fine and dandy for a single person but the problem for many of these blinking retards is that they desire companionship – and this is okay too because the need for companionship is a part of life – but often the people who deal with these blinking retards are doing it for every reason under the sun except love. Again, there goes that deception thing.

Most people have in their minds very descriptive ideas of what a perfect relationship and family life entails. This is one of the reasons why I am against certain shows, like soap operas and certain forms of electronic media. Many people get their ideas of what happy and or perfect relationships are from these sources. If a person who is 'less capable' than most gets it into his or her already twisted mind that this is how life should be, chances are very little else will suffice in making this person happy. This type of thinking is almost guaranteed to cause unhappiness with the significant other because many blinking retards are taught to stick by the person they love at all costs. Now while the 'normal' person is busy taking advantage of the blinking retard for sex, money or whatever gratification is on his or her twisted agenda, the blinking retard is busy with an agenda of his or her very own. That agenda is usually to secure the 'normal' person in the blinking retards life forever.

Be careful, be forewarned and be advised: Many people will lose their damned minds once they engage in good sex! Some men and women, especially if in the first few sexual encounters of their lives or if there has been a significant lapse since the last time they had sex will often become so enchanted by the sex act that they will attach themselves resolutely to the person who provided the orgasmic experience. These people will then often say things like 'I love you' right after the sex act or will try and establish a committed relationship with the other who just wanted to have a physical relationship. It's very hard for certain people to subdue the feelings, which can come along with intercourse thereby causing misunderstood reactions, thereby causing stalkers. These people do however give off certain signs, which will let a prospective sex partner know how possessive and perpetually crazy they will tend to act. One of the biggest signs is –

they will tell you! Some people will come right out and say 'I get crazy when people mess with my feelings' or 'If I find out you're cheating on me, I'll cut your dick off!' and things of that nature. **<u>DO NOT IGNORE THESE SIGNS!</u>** These signs need no explanation and if you're planning to mess with somebody's feelings or planning to cheat, then you deserve whatever consequences, may befall you. However, if your true intentions are displayed and displayed over and over as in 'I don't want a commitment, just a physical relationship' and the other refuses to accept it or accepts what you say and then seems to forget about it after you two have sex, you need to run, screaming, blindly into the night. In other words, you need to just basically extricate yourself from that type of relationship because things will not change - be it due to them having their own agenda, which they cleverly conceal until after the orgasm or be it because they're just borderline crazy. (Cathy) Now I will be the last person in the world to tell you that it's easy to leave a crazy person who provides you with unbelievably wonderful sex but the longer you stay and the more you maintain a physical relationship with that person, the more they will try to turn you into the person or partner they want. Again, the more you have sex with a crazy, the more they will mistakenly think you care about them more than you actually do. What's even more disheartening about this is that over time you may garner such an attraction for them that you may even find yourself making excuses for their actions. What may have started off as I'm just boinking her because people confuse with growing to love someone. This is not growing to love, she has a gorgeous body, can often turn into well she does a lot of stupid shit but…or he's ugly but he does have his good points and so on and so on. This is what many another; this is getting comfortable almost to the point of complacency. What's different and the same is while one person may get 'whipped' after just one night, if the other continues to have his or her sexual fantasies fulfilled night after night, sooner or later, some feelings other than sexual will enter the relationship, especially caring. May take months, may take years but be warned, it'll happen.

Chapter Fifteen
One Final Note About Cheating

Over the last four installments of The Correct Way To Fool Around, I believe I have bestowed upon the general public numerous and invaluable methods of deception which could be used to both detect and deter the act of infidelity. I know that no book in existence details every single method used to perpetrate or counteract the partaking of an affair but I like to believe that with my books on infidelity I have made a miniscule dent in exposing the massive amount of ways. One of the methods which I have used (long before I started writing these books) and have known many people to use when committing infidelity included the use of the words 'hold on.' In my first book, The Correct Way To Fool Around, I touched on how wonderful a thing the invention of the telephone was – especially with the calling features and all. In my first book I also touched on how sneaky some people were and that extreme caution should be exercised at all times when choosing a partner with whom to share or commit your indiscretions. I've noticed however what many people do or should I say don't do is take the necessary time to see if there are any possible connections between one's spouse or significant other and the one with whom they're cheating. If it's a one night stand or a relationship, which has no chance of being anything more than shortly sexual, full disclosure of personal history is not really that necessary or relevant but if the affair is ongoing or has the potential to be long term, you should find out as much as you can about the prospective partner. In this world of massive networking, where one visiting nurse can see dozens of patients and their families in a month, where one computer repair technician can visit the homes of at least twenty to thirty customers a week or where one contract security firm can send an employee to ten different contract locations where there are fifty to five hundred employees at any one particular location over the course of his employment, it's very likely that one person can interact with thousands of people per year. This makes the idea of a person's significant other actually knowing the other person involved in an affair very, very possible. Getting back to the phone, one of the features that many people use is the three way calling and this is the feature, which gets so many people busted in the act of infidelity, it should come with a warning label. What I have noticed people doing is once a person calls, the answering party will tell them to hold on, they will then click over to the free line, call that person's significant other, if known, have them listen in and then reconnect to the original call. Then, when the caller says something incriminating, the caller's significant other can make their presence known or they can wait for more incriminating evidence to pile up so that at their convenience they can let their partner know that they are irrefutably busted! If a person has no evidence on you except circumstantial, meaning nothing that would hold up in any decent argument, you're okay. Now let's recap: if you are cheating with someone and you are not completely sure if they have any connection to your significant other and you call them and they immediately say 'hold on' - hang up the phone. Now because they immediately tell you to hold on, that does not automatically mean they are trying to trap you into saying something incriminating – <u>but it might</u>! Don't take chances. If they call you back later and ask what happened, just say while they had you on hold, you had to answer a call of your own or something creative. Don't doubt your creativity. Remember if you're creative enough to have an affair, you should be creative enough to competently lie about it. Continuing with phones, if you are planning to entertain at your bachelor or bachelorette pad and have a cordless phone, take it off the charger a few hours before your company is scheduled to arrive. Leave the handset off the charger for a sufficient enough amount of time to activate a low battery warning. Reason being, many phones will produce a beep sound when the battery is dead or close to dying. If your significant other happens to call while your natural partner is there, and you were so dumb as not to tell your natural partner you were in a relationship, don't answer the phone or at least have the ringer off and the answering machine's volume turned down until your company leaves. Once they do leave, turn the ringer back on and raise the volume on the answering machine. Do this as soon as they leave because many, if not all cheaters always forget something when it comes to covering their tracks. If later, you call your significant other or they call you and question you about why you didn't pick up the phone, say you were talking to a family member or telemarketer and left the handset on the couch, forgetting to charge it. The beeping sound signaling a dead battery should be reason enough for them to believe you. You may have to create your own excuse for not responding to the answering machine's messages, which they will most certainly leave but you can always say you were in the bathroom – or sleeping.

Here's a question I have for all of you smart people who chose to read my books:

Did you ever notice how kids the world over almost always seem to be spurting the lyrics to some alphabet related or barney/Dora the explorer inspired song? Did you ever wonder why? I did and I found out after careful and honest research that it wasn't because these songs were genetically implanted in their DNA. It was because their parents made it a point to let these little crumb snatchers do nothing but inhale as much of these cartoons and mental conditioning as possible. It made me also wonder about how people generally react when they encounter these children. Usually the reaction is 'oh how cute, they're singing whatever, doing whatever and acting how kids generally act. Can you for one second imagine if these people witnessed these wonderful kids saying fuck you, kiss my ass and things of that nature. These people would simply lose their fucking minds. They would more than likely assume that these poor misguided children have been corrupted by their friends, cable television or by a few misguided family members. They would almost never assume that the parents of these children, the ones who are supposed to provide a loving, positive and supportive environment could be the ones who have corrupted them beyond repair. What many people in this world are unwilling to believe is the fact that those who cheat have many different reasons for doing as they do. Many of these people refuse to think that a child can be influenced by his or her lascivious parents at a very young age –meaning three, four or five and have that level of influence remain with that child up to, into and throughout adulthood. People do not realize that everybody they see on the street is not the person they have always been. Sometimes people turn their lives over to religion – sometimes religious people turn their lives the other way. Sometimes honest people turn into criminals and sometimes criminals turn their lives around and become honest law abiding citizens. When there is a person who commits a sex crime, who just happens to be the son or daughter of a high profile religious icon, it does not mean the high profile religious individual was always so. He or she could have been a low life, sexual deviant scum type of individual who let his son watch x-rated videos as a child twenty or thirty years ago and now that that individual has seen the error of his ways, he no longer does things of that nature but maybe the child does. People are so quick to say 'your parents are sooo nice – how could you be anything but.' However these people have never walked a mile in those parents' moccasins or in the moccasins of the child. Now granted, it is also completely possible that the child could have been influenced by a myriad of other influences, the least of which being the world in general. Some people always expect certain reasons to always be the cause of certain problems. They expect for instance if there's an accident where there is alcohol involved, then the accident is always the fault of the person under the influence. Everybody knows or should know that alcohol is not always the cause of debauchery but it somehow or other always gets the blame. As I mentioned above, people change. Some people change for the better, some people change for the worse. Children who are mentally conditioned to watch and recite these kiddie shows and cartoons when they're young are not always guaranteed to become perfect citizens just as those who sit in front of a TV screen and receive a healthy dose of porn are not guaranteed to become sexual deviants. The problem is that this is the belief of society – and it's not education, which dictates people's actions as much as it is that or those of society. People will be less likely to forgive an indiscretion if all of the reasons the indiscretion was committed are not completely explored. This often makes for an easy out or an easy break up because many times when infidelity is present, people will only focus on the fact that it occurred instead of why and if they do focus on why, it will not be a complete focus - only a scratching of the surface. For some people in this world, this is good because all they care to know is that their significant other was cheating and they are out the door. For the other people this is extremely bad because there are many situations, which resemble infidelity. Infidelity is sitting in a real good position right now because many of the people in this world will never, no matter what, fully explore and investigate it the way it needs to be explored and investigated. Just like there are I believe many people who have been falsely imprisoned, there will I believe be many relationships breaking up either prematurely or permanently due to mistaken beliefs due to infidelity.

To keep a cheating relationship under wraps, people need to be cold. They need to be able to see the person they are cheating with and not speak, not look at them, basically ignore them especially if it's a workplace romance type of situation. The problem with this is that many people, especially women are not experts at being cold. Don't get me wrong – women reign supreme when it comes to dishing out evilness after someone does them wrong but if it comes to just acting mean, few of them can accomplish it. They let their emotions get in the way. They just have to say hi or give that little nod of acknowledgement or something that may give away the fact they are doing something bad. People have to give the impression that there is no possible way to make any possible connection between the person they're cheating with and that person's significant other. This does not take practice as much as it does concentration. It takes concentrating on ignoring all home training. It takes looking at the person you are sleeping with like ' oh fuck, here comes this bitch again.' It's not a point of acting; it is a point of deception. It is the same level of deception as the initial cheating act. It is not easy to do. I say this because when a person indulges in good sex, it is extremely difficult to see the other party as anything other than someone who makes that person feel good. A person committing infidelity has to do everything in his or her power to distance himself or herself from the one he or she is cheating with. This includes but is not limited to badmouthing this person behind his or her back. People usually badmouth somebody they do not like. Think about it – when was the last time you heard someone say 'I can't stand that motherfucker' and then see that person go hang out with the person she said she couldn't stand. You don't. You know why? It's because when a person expresses extreme dislike for another, the only time the person expressing the dislike will be nice to that person is to make that person or other people believe that he or she is being deceptive and trying to make people think other than what exists. This also includes flirting with someone else in the presence of the one you are cheating with. This more than likely will give everybody around you the impression that you are interested in someone other than who you actually are but it may also cause friction between you and the person you are cheating with. This is where budgeting time and complete honesty come into play. You have to not only allow enough time between the significant other and the person you are cheating with but you have to allow enough time to flirt with other people so that the likelihood of your indiscretion will be lessened. The complete honesty part is solely for the benefit of the natural partner. You must be honest enough with him or her so that he or she knows that your flirting is nothing more than a diversionary tactic – and if worst case scenario the flirting goes a little bit too far, then the natural partner should be secure enough to know that he or she will still be number one outside of the significant other and that whatever happened between the two was nothing more than further diversion.

Well that's it. No more correct way to fool around, no more infidelity secrets and no more controversial, argument starting topics. My initial goal in writing the correct way to fool around was to teach people to be wary of the tricks and deception, which came along with infidelity. I hope that I have in some small stretch of the imagination accomplished that goal. I know that there are many more tricks pertaining to the field of infidelity yet to be discovered and I also know that there are many folks who dislike me because of what I have chosen to write about and I do apologize if I have offended anyone with the content contained within. It was never my intention to offend. It was however to inform. As far as the undiscovered tricks pertaining to the world of infidelity, I will definitely keep my eyes and ears open and if I so happen to come across anything new or anything that haven't covered in my books which I feel might be of particular interest to you infidelity knowledge seekers, I will surely include them in an upcoming publication. Until then please enjoy my present publications. If you have already, then offer them to someone who may be in need of a little enlightenment as well as a little laughter.

Thank you from

Jeremiah Dotson

Author of

THE CORRECT WAY TO FOOL AROUND

THE CORRECT WAY TO FOOL AROUND PART TWO

THE CORRECT WAY TO FOOL AROUND PART THREE

THE CORRECT WAY TO FOOL AROUND PART FOUR

RELATIONSHIPS; PACIFICATION FOR CRAZY PEOPLE

VICTIMS OF CIRCUMSTANCE

End for now…

Made in the USA
Charleston, SC
10 July 2010